HOW TO TEACH FRENCH PHONETICS

Lessons, Exercises & Drills
For Class Use

BY

BATEMAN

Diplômé d'Etudes Supérieures; Docteur de l'Université de Caen; Chief Modern Language Master, Reading School.

AND

J. E THORNTON, M.A. (OXON)

Senior Modern Language Master, Leeds Boys Modern School

CAMBRIDGE:
W. HEFFER & SONS LTD
1921

WARNER MEMORIAL LIBRARY
EASTERN UNIVERSITY
ST. DAVIDS, PA 19087-3696

12/15/09

PC 2135 .B3 2009
Bateman, Gerald Cooper.
How to teach French
 phonetics

How to Teach French Phonetics

Bateman

Copyright © BiblioLife, LLC

BiblioLife Reproduction Series: Our goal at BiblioLife is to help readers, educators and researchers by bringing back in print hard-to-find original publications at a reasonable price and, at the same time, preserve the legacy of literary history. The following book represents an authentic reproduction of the text as printed by the original publisher and may contain prior copyright references. While we have attempted to accurately maintain the integrity of the original work(s), from time to time there are problems with the original book scan that may result in minor errors in the reproduction, including imperfections such as missing and blurred pages, poor pictures, markings and other reproduction issues beyond our control. Because this work is culturally important, we have made it available as a part of our commitment to protecting, preserving and promoting the world's literature.

All of our books are in the "public domain" and some are derived from Open Source projects dedicated to digitizing historic literature. We believe that when we undertake the difficult task of re-creating them as attractive, readable and affordable books, we further the mutual goal of sharing these works with a larger audience. A portion of BiblioLife profits go back to Open Source projects in the form of a donation to the groups that do this important work around the world. If you would like to make a donation to these worthy Open Source projects, or would just like to get more information about these important initiatives, please visit www.bibliolife.com/opensource.

PREFACE.

THE following pages are not concerned with Phonetic Theory. They deal with practice, and with practice confined to the elementary stages in the class-room. They are the result of actual class-room experience.

The book has been divided into two parts : the first part containing a course of ten introductory lessons for teaching the phonetic symbols, and the second part being devoted to a collection of class-room exercises, described below.

PART I. THE TEACHING OF THE FRENCH PHONETIC SYMBOLS.

The amount of phonetic theory that should be taught in the modern-language classes of our schools will long remain a point of contention among modern-language masters : teachers differ widely in their practice in this respect. We have therefore adopted the plan of giving two sets of introductory lessons for teaching the phonetic symbols—the first set representing what in our opinion should be the *minimum*, and the second set, the *maximum* of phonetic theory taught. This plan will allow the reader to choose the one he prefers, or to substitute for either set a combination or modification of both.

There is, moreover, no reason why the matter contained in the series of introductory lessons should not

PREFACE

be spread over 15 or 20 periods, instead of 10 or 12, if the teacher prefers to take his class more slowly. Unless he has had previous experience in teaching phonetics it will probably be advisable for him to adopt this course.

PART II CLASS-ROOM EXERCISES IN FRENCH PHONETICS.

(1) EAR-TRAINING EXERCISES (Series A):

These exercises are designed to practise the class in *recognising* and *distinguishing between* the various French sounds. It is obviously impossible for a pupil to reproduce a sound until he is capable of hearing it correctly.

(2) ARTICULATION EXERCISES (Series B).

The exercises grouped under this heading are designed to practise the class in *reproducing* the single French sounds, once they have been clearly distinguished.

(3) SOUND-DRILLS (Series C):

The exercises of this series are designed to practise the class in various *combinations* of sounds after they have become proficient in reproducing them singly

(4) PRELIMINARY EXERCISES IN PHONETIC READING AND DICTATION (Series D).

Series A, B and C provide material for that preparatory work which is essential before the class can cope successfully with the phonetic text of their reading book.

Moreover, for many months after this preliminary

PREFACE vii

stage is passed, it will be found advisable to devote from five to eight minutes of each period to the exercises given in these series. Without this constant drilling in the sounds and their various combinations the accent of the class will tend gradually to deteriorate.

The exercises of Series D are designed to introduce the pupils gradually to the reading and writing of consecutive phonetic texts. They will consequently not be required until the class has spent several weeks practising the exercises of Series A, B and C.

How to Use the Exercises.

The basic idea of the method here advocated is the 10 *minute unit*.

The exercises of Series A and B are designed to last 10 minutes—some may be extended to 15 minutes if desired, and a few short exercises of 2 or 3 minutes duration have been included, but the unit aimed at throughout is the 10 minute exercise. The Sound-drills of Series C are arranged on a phonetic basis and not according to the time taken in saying them : from 4 to 5 of the drills can be worked through thoroughly in the space of ten minutes.

It is suggested that variety is essential in the teaching of phonetics, and that to obtain this variety each lesson should be composed of from 4 to 6 different exercises, lasting from 5 to 10 minutes each. The advantage of grouping the exercises under the headings :

        A. Ear-training (16 exercises)
        B. Articulation (10 ,,)
        C. Sound-drills (38 ,,)

is that it allows the teacher a perfectly free hand for composing each lesson as he thinks best for the particular needs of the class he is taking. Variety in practice may thus be combined with definiteness of aim.

Thus, in the early stages, when the class is learning to distinguish between the different French sounds, Series A will predominate : but Series B will soon be required to practise the class in reproducing the easier sounds they will have already learnt to distinguish. The lessons at this stage will consequently take the form of A–B–A–B–A (*i.e.* 3 exercises from Series A alternating with 2 from Series B).

Later, when the class has learnt to recognise most of the sounds, the chief attention will be given to reproduction. The lessons at this stage will consequently take the form of B–A–B–A–B (*i.e.* 3 exercises from Series B alternating with 2 from Series A).

As the consonant sounds are added to the vowel-sounds, and the class is gaining proficiency in reproducing the vowel-sounds, the Sound-drills will gradually come into use. Towards the fourth week the lessons may thus take the form of A–B–C–B–C (*i.e.* 2 exercises from Series B alternating with 2 from Series C, after one exercise from Series A).

When it is remembered that A represents a choice of 16 different exercises ; B a choice of 10 ; and C a choice of 38, it will be seen that the amount of variety offered by this method is very great, while the division into the three series assures of the desired balance always being maintained, in any given lesson, between the different aims.

A sample set of five lessons, designed for practising the vowel-symbols before the consonant-symbols have been taught, is given on page 43 ; these lessons, however, are given merely as an example of possible combinations—many other arrangements would do equally well. As an instance of the extreme variety which may be introduced into a single lesson on the method here advocated, the reader is referred to the sample lesson given on the following page.

We shall be grateful for any suggestions from teachers which may add to the usefulness of this little book.

The Sound-drills are published separately for class use.

G. C. B.
J. E. T.

MODEL LESSON.

(*Time :* 45 *minutes.*)

Class repeat all the vowel-symbols, as indicated in B 8 (*last paragraph*)	¼ min.
Class repeat exercise : B 5	½ ,,
Teacher dictates 10 sounds : A 7	10 ,,
Class (standing) sing sound-scale : B 7 ..	1 ,,
Class read (after teacher) :	
C. Sound-drills 4 and 6	4 ,,
,, 2 and 7	4 ,,
Class read (alone) 3 lines each of :	
C. Sound-drills 20, 21, 23	5 ,,
,, 11, 13, 15	5 ,,
Pupil dictates 5 sounds : A 14	5 ,,
Eliminatory exercises : B 10	10 ,,
Class repeat exercise : B 8	¼ ,,

———————

This actual amount and variety of work has frequently been accomplished in a single lesson, once the class have become familiar with the exercises. The division of the lesson into minutes is of course only approximative. It is, however, possible to get through each of the separate exercises thoroughly, and without hurrying, in the time assigned to it, and to complete the whole of them, as here given, within the 45 minutes.

The lesson contains 6 different exercises and 10 different sound-drills. The Series alternate thus: B-B-A-B-C-C-A-B-B.

    A. (ear-training) receives 15 minutes.
    B. (articulation) ,, 12 ,,
    C. (sound-drills) ,, 18 ,,

This division would be suitable for a class that had been doing phonetics for about a month.

CONTENTS

PART I.
THE TEACHING OF THE FRENCH PHONETIC SYMBOLS.

	PAGE
FIRST SERIES (12 LESSONS)	2-19
SECOND SERIES (10 LESSONS)	20-56

PART II.
CLASS-ROOM EXERCISES IN FRENCH PHONETICS.

(A.) EAR-TRAINING EXERCISES	59
(B.) ARTICULATION EXERCISES	69
(C.) SOUND DRILLS	75
(D.) PRELIMINARY EXERCISES IN PHONETIC READING AND DICTATION	88

PART I.

THE TEACHING OF THE FRENCH
PHONETIC SYMBOLS.

THE TEACHING OF THE FRENCH SOUNDS.

FIRST SERIES (12 LESSONS).

LESSON 1.

APPARATUS :— Dents' Wall Chart —"Les Sons du Français."

A set of Sound Charts (Tongue and Lip Positions), Jones and Rausch (Dent & Sons)

Yellow Chalk for phonetic symbols

White Chalk for ordinary writing. Mirrors.

1. The teacher will say that all sounds in French differ from English sounds, chiefly in tensity—explain tenseness by demonstration. When an English person says " i " there is no spreading of lips, no movement of stiffening of the throat, for the French " i," the lips are widely spread, the head is pushed forward, and the wind-pipe stiffens. Class note and make a similar demonstration.

Blackboard : i   e
            (1)   (2)

4   HOW TO TEACH FRENCH PHONETICS

Repeat three times each.

i	e	u	o
(1)	(2)	(8)	(7)

Repeat 8 and 7 three times each.

Repeat three times 1, 2, 8, 7.

2. The Class will recognise the sounds by means of the numbers which they will call out to the teacher.

Each pupil will only call out one number; if the teacher hears a wrong number called he will make the distinction of the sounds thus:—

This is No. 1 = i, i, i, i.
          No. 2 = e, e, e, e.

Do you hear the difference?   i e, i e, i e.

Any other difficulties?

3. Call attention to chart and write on board:—

i	(1)
e	(2)
ɛ	(3)
a	(4)

Tell class to watch lip movement for these four sounds:

  i   e   ɛ   a

What happens?   The lips open.

When are they most closed?   For No. 1.

When are they most open?   For No. 4.

FRENCH PHONETIC SYMBOLS   5

Draw the shape of the lips for No. 1 on the board, Jones :—

Teacher : This is called the close position.

∴ By questions to pupils

"a" is called the open position.

The following FRONT VOWELS will then be written on the left of the board, thus :—

Corners of lips pulled back, tightly spread.

Top and bottom lips are :—

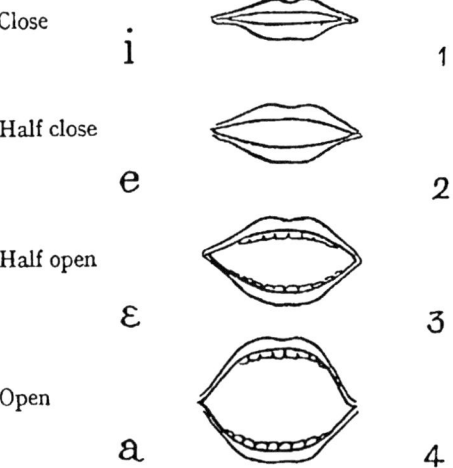

Repeat three times and recognise as in paragraph 2.

6 HOW TO TEACH FRENCH PHONETICS

4. The same procedure will be adopted for the Back Vowels.

The following BACK VOWELS will then be added on the right of the blackboard thus:—

Lips pushed forward, rounded, and

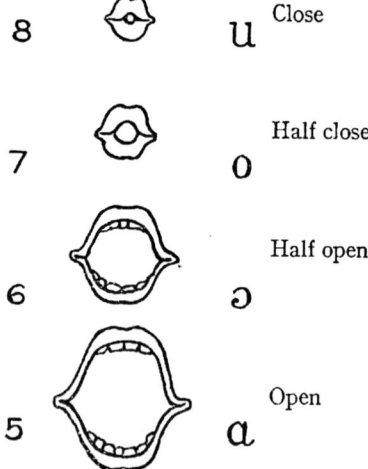

NOTE.—The numbers of the vowel sounds should be written on the Wall Chart, in coloured chalk, against each symbol. This chart should be hung in front of the class and be kept there during the whole of the phonetic training.

5. Mirrors: "u" position, lips far forward as possible, rounded and closed. Tell class to *think* of " u " in fool, boot, and to say after teacher: u, u, u, u.

FRENCH PHONETIC SYMBOLS 7

No Lip Quivering of Any Kind.

Explain that movement of lips alters the sound produced ; demonstate by saying " i " and moving the lips right forward, they will hear quite a different sound—similarly " o " moved, adds on an " u " sound giving a double sound, or dipthong " ou " which is English and must never be made in French.

Repeat again and often—" No lip quivering."

Repeat u, u, u, u. Class will do so. Then they will try " u," " o " each time after the teacher, keeping the same lip position and pitching up the sound " o " which will at first sound stifled.

This does not matter.

6. Hints. For " u " tell the class to make the sound softly and not to force the breath through the mouth. Also if they do not get a pure " u " sound or a good " o " sound tell them to touch their bottom teeth with the tip of the tongue and then to feel backwards as far as they can—keep the tongue still in this position and repeat sound. This will have the effect of raising the back of the tongue to the right height.

Another hint for " o " is to place a pencil about 1 inch in the mouth and close the lips round the pencil. This has the effect of making the tongue rise towards the back and closes the lips to a good rounded position.

7. The Charts of the Back Vowels will be hung at the back of the class room. The front vowels in front of the class in the following order :—1 2 3.

Nos. 9 and 10 will be added later
    under 1 and 2, thus :—9, 10.

8   HOW TO TEACH FRENCH PHONETICS

End of lesson repeat all sounds over again in order :—

    1, 2, 3, 4.   8, 7, 6, 5.

and do some recognition.

Preparation —Practice at home, *with mirrors* :—

    i, u, o.

LESSON 2.

1. Lesson 1 will be gone through again pointing to the symbols on the chart (against which numbers must be put); repeat each sound three times in the following order :—1 2 3 4 8 7 6 5, after which they will be said straight through once.

2. Recognition by numbers.

3. Mirrors :—Lip position for No. 1. Lips tightly spread—repeat each time after teacher, i, i, i.

Tell them to force the head forward when making the sound; stiffen the wind pipe.

Then after teacher practise   i e, i e, without changing the lip position.

The following orders may well be given when it is desired to teach No. 2 vowel sound " e " :—

Take up glasses.

  Lean back in your seats so that I can see your lips.

  Keep your eyes fixed on your glasses and *don't* look at me either before, during, or after the sound.

FRENCH PHONETIC SYMBOLS

No. 1 position :

Corners well back.

Top and bottom lips close together, the teeth slightly apart

Press tongue hard against lower teeth.

Now think of " i " and imitate the sound I am making — e, e, e, e, e, e, e.

Relax.

Now when you make this sound the only lip movement must be a sideways one. Try and pull the corners of your lips back while you make the sound Don't let the top and bottom lips separate further while you make the sound.

Force the head forward a little.

It will be necessary frequently to tell them to pitch up the sound.

LESSON 3.

Repeat as in Lesson 2, (1) (2).

Practise as in Lesson 1 (5), 2 (3).

1. Write up on the board y (9)

ø (10),

and hang up Sound Charts 9, 10, as indicated in Lesson 1.

Make the sounds three times.

10 HOW TO TEACH FRENCH PHONETICS

2. EXPLANATION.

Ask for lip position :—

Tell the class that the sound is very easy to produce. The lip position of 8, and the tongue position of 1. That is to say, if they put their lips in the position of " u " and try to say " i " the result will be " y " No 9. This is called a mixed vowel, because it has properties of both the front and back vowels.

Similarly No. 10 has the lip position of 7, and the tongue position of 2.

3. PRACTICE :—With lip position of 8 say 1.

(a) Then try slowly exercise which teacher will supervise as follows :—

With glasses—say No. 1.

Lips forward to No. 8 position

Keep this position and say No. 1.

Continue the exercise thus :—

Back—say No. 1.

Forward—say No. 1

(b) Class with lip position of " o " will repeat after teacher the sound " e " made very sharply six times.

4. DIFFICULTIES

Any pupil who cannot pronounce " y " as indicated above may be told to push his tongue forward into the hollow made by pushing the lips forward, and then try to say " i." Similar indication for " ø " from " e."

Preparation ·—Practise sounds and positions as indicated.

FRENCH PHONETIC SYMBOLS

LESSON 4.

Teacher will repeat 1 2 3 4; 8 7 6 5; 1 and 9; 2 and 10. Three times each sound except 1 and 9, and 2 and 10, which will be made in groups three times each group.

1. Dictate ten sounds. The class will write down the symbols, *never* the number of the sound dictated. Correct on blackboard and distinguish between the sounds which have proved difficult to the class—always in the manner outlined in Lesson 1. (2).

2. Exercise with class " i " " e " for about 3 mins.
   ,,   ,,   " u " " o "   ,,   ,,
   ,,   ,,   " i " " y "   ,,   ,,
   ,,   ,,   " ø "   twelve times.

The above with some individuals, and in chorus

3. The sound ε will now be taught.

Mirrors :—Class will study lip position of teacher and try to reproduce the position by means of their mirrors.

The teacher will check positions and will then tell the class to think of the word " get " and imitate the sound ε, ε, ε, ε. No lip or tongue movement.

4. Open the mouth to full extent and from the front of the tongue produce the sound a, a, a, a.

NOTE.—The class must be warned that if they do not open their mouths wide they will have a sound between 3 and 4, which is " æ " as in hat, man

5. DRILL. In position of I, say after teacher "ɪ" "e," open mouth ! after teacher ɛ, open wider ! after teacher "a."

6. Preparation : Practise as indicated in 5 :—

    ɪ   e   ɛ   a

LESSON 5.

1. The teacher will repeat sounds as usual and dictate ten.

2. Practise as in Lesson 4 (5) then i, y, and ø, u, o.

3. Pupils will now be taught ɔ, ɑ. These will be written on the board ɔ(6), ɑ(5).

Lips rounded and half-opened. Position copied from teacher. Class will be told to think of the sound in the word "nut" and pronounce the sound after teacher ɔ, ɔ, ɔ. Lips must be kept rounded

4. Mouth wide open—sound of "a" in "father" but produced slightly more forward—after teacher ɑ, ɑ, ɑ, ɑ.

5. EXPLANATION.

The teacher will pronounce clearly a, ɑ, several times and demonstrate the difference between No. 4 and No. 5

He will draw a diagram on the board and mark the point from which the sound appears to leave the tongue for æ, a, ɑ.

6. Repeat twice all sounds learnt.

Class will practise these for preparation.

FRENCH PHONETIC SYMBOLS

LESSON 6

To be a resumé of the previous lessons. The teacher making the sounds.

Dictating ten sounds.

Distinguishing between sounds which have been muddled.

Getting each pupil in turn to the chart, and seeing if he can pick out correctly three sounds made. Those who cannot pass are moved to the front of the class for special attention.

A second dictation of ten sounds.

LESSON 7.

Class will repeat after the teacher

ı	e	ɛ	a
u	o	ɔ	ɑ
i	y		
e	ø		

Plenty of drill in these sounds, and individual attention and two or three dictations of ten sounds.

The sound ə will be taught.

Tell the class to say e ø then with lips unrounded repeat ø which gives ə This must not be lengthened into ə:, it is a light sound.

The third dictation of ten sounds should be at the end of the lesson, after which the teacher will repeat the sounds before dismissing the class.

14 HOW TO TEACH FRENCH PHONETICS

LESSON 8.

Drill and dictation as usual

The sound " œ " will be taught.

Mirrors : With lip rounding of No. 6 say No. 3

A further drill and dictation of sounds.

Revision of previous lessons by means of questions and answers. Description of lip positions by various pupils.

A further test as described in Lesson 6.

LESSON 9.

Drill and dictation of sounds.

Nasalised vowels.

Mirrors :—The teacher will tell the pupils to say the sound " m " with their fingers placed on the part of the nose where the hard bone ends They will be asked if they feel a vibration. It will then be remarked that certain sounds are made through the nose, others through the mouth. They will be told that in French there are four nasalised vowel sounds.

Before proceeding with the lesson and explaining how the sounds are made, recourse should be had to the " Organs of Speech " chart and the movement of the soft palate described when (ɑ) and (ɑ̃) are made.

The class will now hear the teacher make the nasalised

FRENCH PHONETIC SYMBOLS

vowels which will be put up on the blackboard and numbered thus:—

ɑ̃ ɔ̃ ɛ̃ œ̃
(14) (15) (13) (16)

Each sound will be repeated three times.

Recognition by numbers will follow.

ɑ̃ will now be taught.

Mouth at No. 5 position with fingers on nose to feel the buzzing. Say ɑ̃ through the nose and mouth.

5. They must be taught to make this sound in No. 7 position. Great care must always be taken that the position for 14 is open 5, and the position for 15 is closed 7.

This is especially important for English people who tend to produce an open 6 nasalised which they use for either 14 or 15.

Dictation of ten sounds introducing two or three times ɑ̃ and ɔ̃

Preparation:—Practise sounds.

LESSON 10.

DRILL AND DICTATION.

In teaching No. 13 reference should be made to Lesson 5, paragraph 5, and the class told that ɛ̃ is really æ nasalised. It is frequently better to work from this starting point.

Teach 13 and 16 as indicated in Lesson 9. When 13 has been mastered, the same sound produced with rounded lips will give 16. Care must be taken not to get a tin(ny) sound for No. 13. It should be soft.

Drill and Dictation.

The teacher will repeat the sounds in the order as under, two or three times. After this lesson they will always be repeated thus at the commencement and end of each class :—

        i   e   ɛ   a   u   o   ɔ   ɑ
        i   y
        e   ø
        ɛ   œ
        ɑ̃   ɔ̃   ɛ̃   œ̃

(With clear lip movement.)

i a y, i a y, continued until sign made to stop.

NOTE.—All these exercises mentioned must be repeated until the class is thoroughly conversant with the sounds, particularly the exercise Lesson 4 (2) with the addition of e ø, ɛ œ.

When 50 per cent. of the class can take down ten sounds correctly, the whole class can learn the consonants.

THE CONSONANTS.

LESSON 11.

During all the lessons on the consonants, the daily vowel drill, dictation, and recognition by numbers must be carried out twice during each lesson. Consonants as learned may be added to the vowel sounds when 80 per cent. of the class can take down ten vowel sounds correctly.

The teacher will first make the class understand the difference between the term "voiced"—"unvoiced."

The consonants f v will be taken as examples.

    f will be made 5 times.

    v   ,,   ,,   ,,

The class will be told to say " f " with the fingers on the front of the throat. The difference when they make the " v " will be automatically demonstrated.

They will then be told that consonants are in pairs, voiced—unvoiced ; these will be pointed out on the chart.

The sign under a symbol, thus $_\circ$ means that the sound is unvoiced.

The " r."

This is a most important sound. French cannot be spoken unless some kind of " r " is made—the teacher should demonstrate   R   R$_\circ$

       r   r̥

18 HOW TO TEACH FRENCH PHONETICS

Diagrams should be drawn to show how the uvular and the lingual R are made Anyone who cannot make some kind of R must practise one or both of the following exercises :—

(1) To produce a uvular R, gargle daily with water, gradually reducing the amount until a gargle can be made without water.

(2) To produce a lingual r, say tədətədə for about 5 minutes daily ; then practise words such as dry, drop, drum, try, etc., making an effort to vibrate the tongue.

The teacher will choose the sound which the pupil makes the better and tell him always to make use of that one.

LESSON 12.

Drill and Dictation of vowel sounds.

Dictation of isolated consonant sounds.

The sounds l, l̥ will now be attempted.

The teacher will tell the class to say the English word " will ", then putting the front of the tongue well forward against the top gums and pressing the point upwards prolong the last sound of the word will—ll—ll. This is the French l. They will then make the breathed l̥. It should be pointed out that the " ll " used in the word " ball " for example, is never used in French ; this sound is called a dark " l " because it is produced far back, and is indistinct.

FRENCH PHONETIC SYMBOLS

j is learned by the class being taught to isolate the first sound of the word " yes."

ɲ is learned in a similar way by means of the word " onion."

w lips brought forward to No. 8 position and back to No. 1, saying the sound of the letter " w " in " what."

The breathed " ɥ " is made with the same lip position with breath only, and is almost a breathed (unvoiced) whistle.

When the class can get 80 per cent. marks on the vowels and consonants isolated and in combination, five lessons will be devoted to the exercises on Ear-training and Articulation.

No other exercises should be attempted until 95 or 100 per cent. marks can be obtained on vowels and consonants.

Afterwards the Sound Drills may be used by the pupils on the lines explained in the Preface.

Great care must be taken that all consonants, and particularly final consonants, are well and clearly made. In French, consonants and vowel sounds are made with more effort and precision than in English. The sound must be a definite one, made and completed, leaving no trace of any additional intermediate sound. This is the most important part of the elementary phonetic reading.

When complete fluency with all the various types of exercises has been obtained, the class can proceed to phonetic reading and dictation. (*Vide* Series D.)

THE TEACHING OF THE FRENCH SOUNDS.

SECOND SERIES (10 LESSONS).

All these lessons are given in English.
Yellow chalk is used for all symbols.
Each lesson lasts 45 minutes.

LESSON 1.

1. The 8 normal vowel-sounds: *Tongue positions*.

" Before learning to speak French we must learn to pronounce the French sounds; we cannot use our English sounds, for the French use quite different ones. Have you ever heard a Frenchman speaking English ? Did it sound funny ? Why ? " Master imitates a Frenchman saying—it is very difficult. " Just as a Frenchman sounds absurd if he speaks English with the French sounds, so an Englishman sounds absurd if he tries to speak French with our English sounds."

" To-day we shall start with 8 vowel-sounds, and we shall see especially how the tongue is placed in pronouncing them."

" Each of these sounds has a special sign—called a *symbol*—and we shall always use yellow chalk for these sound-symbols so as to avoid mixing them up with the ordinary letters."

FRENCH PHONETIC SYMBOLS

" It will help us to have a diagram of the mouth, so as to be able to show the different tongue-positions." (B.B.1.) The teacher draws diagram and explains it.

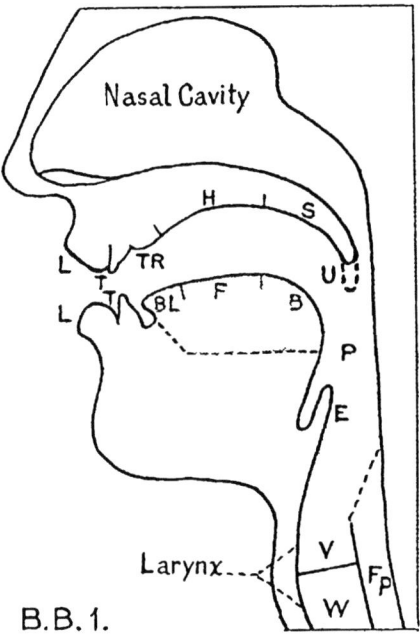

B.B. 1.

" Now will you all say the word " eat," and while you are saying it put your little finger in between your teeth and tell me where your tongue is? Is it near the front teeth or at the back of the mouth? Near the teeth? Good. Now start again, but this time while you are saying " eat," and your little finger is touching your tongue, suddenly change to ' oo '."

"What happens? The tongue has disappeared? That's right. But where has it gone to? Take a good breath, say " oo " again, and while you are saying it push your little finger slowly into your mouth till you come to your tongue. Have you found it? Where is it? Right at the back? That's right."

"Now let me show you on the blackboard the position of the tongue for the sound " ee " and for " oo." The French sound for (i) is tighter than this English sound, but we shall talk about that later; the French sound for (u) is much the same as the English sound (fool)."

The teacher draws in tongue position for (i) (B B.1) and for (u) (B.B.2). He explains that the symbol is placed at the highest point reached by the tongue, forward and back.

"Now take your glasses and say ' cart.' Where is the tongue now? Lying flat at the bottom? Can any boy draw me the position on the diagram?" The pupil draws it in, teacher correcting. "This French sound is more or less like the English one. The tongue is raised highest at the back, so we place the symbol (ɑ) here." The teacher draws it in (B.B.3).

"Now I am going to say a sound that does not exist in English (except in some dialects), and you must watch my tongue and say where it rises highest. I shall begin by saying (ɑ) and then say the new sound, so watch the movement of my tongue." The teacher says (ɑ, a), (ɑ, a), (ɑ, a), so that the class can see the movement of his tongue, and asks a pupil to draw in the new position; he corrects and writes in (a). (B.B.4.) "You must notice that this sound is lower than the sound in English in the word ' cat,' for instance. if I say the word ' cat ' with the French sound it would be (kat). The tongue is still flat, but it is slightly raised in front."

i B.B.1.

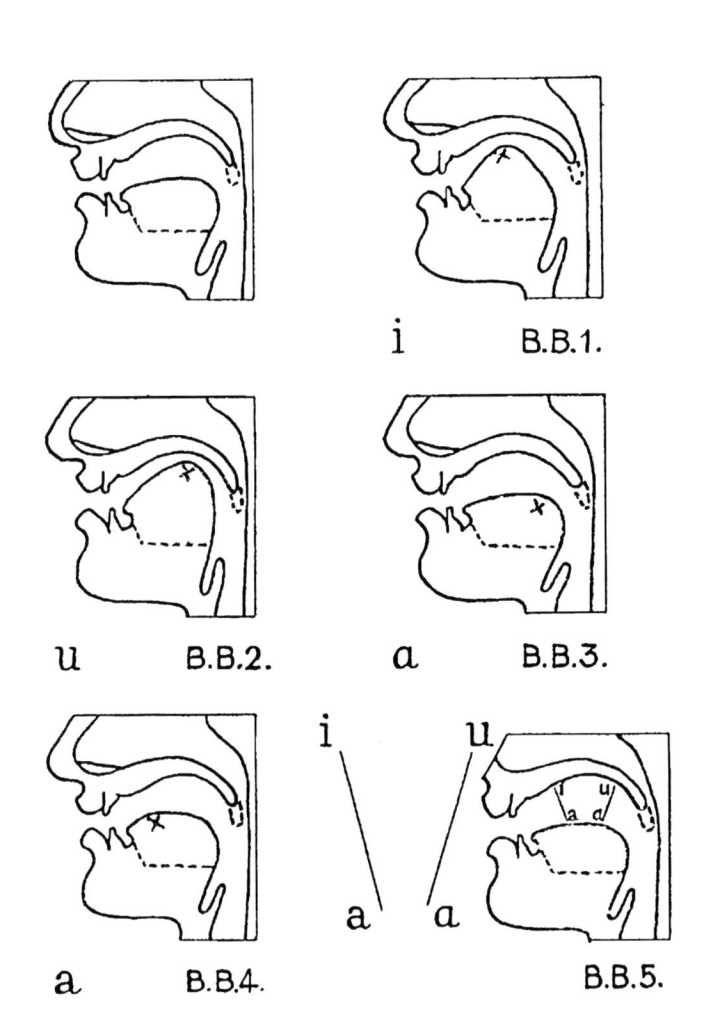

u B.B.2.

a B.B.3.

a B.B.4.

B.B.5.

"Now you must notice these four tongue positions · (i) is the sound made when the tongue is in the highest position forward, (a) when it is in the lowest position forward; (u) is the sound made when the tongue is in the highest position back, (ɑ) when it is in the lowest position back. Let us make a figure on the blackboard of these four points, and join (i) and (a); and (u) and (ɑ) (B.B.5.)"

"Between (i) and (a) there are two sounds; that is to say there are two sounds in saying which the tongue is raised forward not so high as for (i), but higher than for (a); these two sounds are (e)," [marking it in], "and (ɛ)," [marking it in]; "the symbol being placed in each case at the point reached by the tongue."

"Between (u) and (ɑ) there are also two sounds; these two sounds are (o) and (ɔ)," [marking them in], "each symbol being placed at the point reached by the tongue. As you see, the tongue is raised at the back for these sounds."

"We have now a figure like this (B.B.6). These are the eight sounds we have to learn to-day."

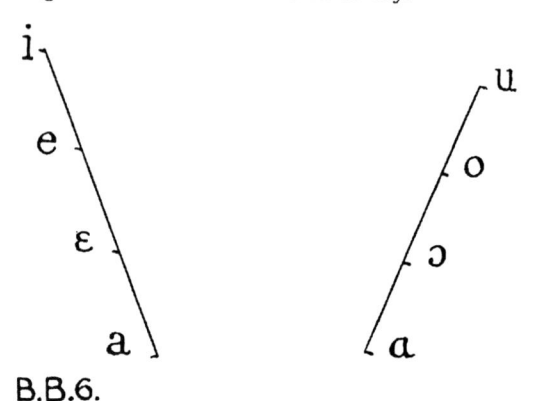

i
e
ɛ
a

u
o
ɔ
ɑ

B.B.6.

FRENCH PHONETIC SYMBOLS 25

" Starting from the top position of the tongue forward, and reading down to the bottom position forward, we have (i, e, ε, a) ; starting from the top position of the tongue back, and reading down to the bottom position back, we have (u, o, ɔ, ɑ). In both cases the tongue descends and the mouth opens a little more for each sound, as one goes from top to bottom."

The teacher then reads the symbols (i, e, ε, a) and (u, o, ɔ, ɑ) several times slowly through, pointing to each as he says it.

He then asks questions on the lesson : " Why are there two lines ? Why is (e) placed above (ε) ; is the tongue higher when I say (ε) than it is when I say (ɔ) No , then what is the difference ? Which sounds are made with the tongue at the back of the mouth ? Why is (i) called a forward sound ? How would you describe the position of (u) ? " etc.

The teacher then rubs out diagrams and places a diagram of the mouth on blackboard. He calls on various pupils to fill in the different tongue-positions of the sounds he calls out.

LESSON 2

2. The 8 normal vowel-sounds . *Lip-positions*.

" In the last lesson we learnt the tongue-positions for the eight normal vowel-sounds. To-day we shall go through the same sounds again, but with special reference to their lip-positions.

" The position of the lips is more important than that of the tongue ; it is chiefly because the French

26 HOW TO TEACH FRENCH PHONETICS

use their lips much more than the English that their language is hard for us to learn. For many of the French sounds we shall have to put our lips into positions we never use in English.

"But first let us run through the last lesson again." Ten minutes are given to recapitulation. (B.B.1.)

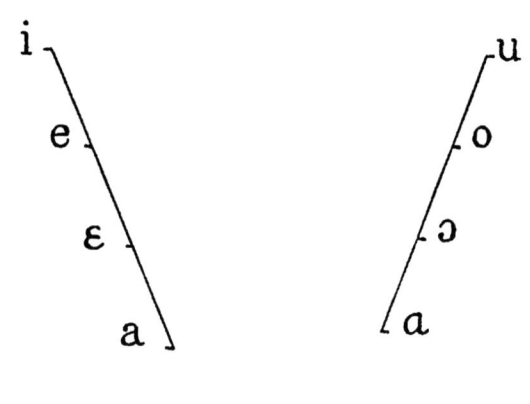

```
        i               u
        e               o
        ɛ               ɔ
        a               ɑ
```

B.B.1.

"Now for the position of the lips. It is essential to know the right lip-positions and to put your lips into them, which is not at all easy at first. I am going to say the four front vowel-sounds from top to bottom, five times, and then I shall call one of you out to draw the position of my lips on the blackboard." The teacher does so, and a pupil writes the lip-positions at the side of the symbols on the blackboard. "Now I shall do the same for the back vowels." A pupil writes

FRENCH PHONETIC SYMBOLS

these positions at the side of the symbols. The teacher controls this work and corrects where necessary, as far as possible with the help of the class. (B.B.2.)

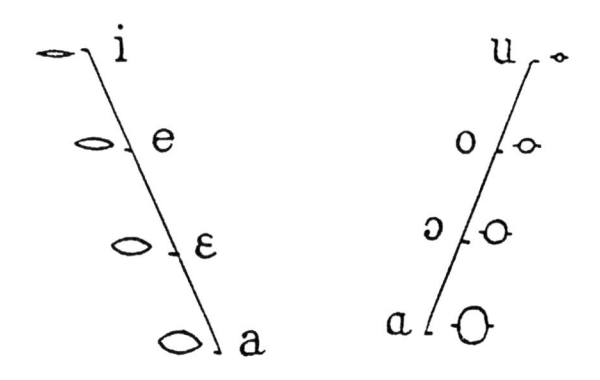

B.B.2.

"Now the first thing to notice is that the lips are stretched tight for (ı) and (e), and open out for (ɛ) and (a); the front vowels have the stretched form of lips; while for (u) and (o) the lips are tightly rounded, opening out for (ɔ) and (ɑ); the back vowels have the rounded form of lips. The front vowels have stretched lips; the back vowels rounded lips.

"Then another important point to notice, is that once the lips are in the right position, *they do not move at all*, but remain in the same position all the time the sound is being said.

28 HOW TO TEACH FRENCH PHONETICS

"This is very important to remember for (e) and (o), because in English we move our lips when saying these sounds. Listen to me saying them and try to find out if the sound changes at the end, and into what it changes." The teacher then pronounces "gay" and "go," and elicits (ei) and (ou). He explains the double nature of these sounds; remarks on the movement of the lips while saying them; he demonstrates the French sounds again, telling the class to notice that his lips don't move at all while saying them.

The teacher then exercises the class in lip-positions. He reads down the front vowels (i, e, ε, a) and the back ones (u, o, ɔ, ɑ), keeping the lips the same for the two top sounds in each case and dropping the jaw distinctly for (ε) (ɔ) and again for (a) (ɑ) He then tells the class to take their glasses in their hands and imitate him, controlling their lip-movement by the glass.

The class is exercised thus (lip-movement only, no sound) :—

The teacher says (i)–(e), keeping the lips in the same position; the class put their lips in position.

,, ,, ,, (ε), distinctly dropping his lower jaw; the class take up the new lip-position

,, ,, ,, (a), again distinctly dropping the jaw; the class take up the new lip-position.

This process is repeated for the back vowels.

The teacher goes through these sounds several times.

FRENCH PHONETIC SYMBOLS 29

He then asks the class to put their lips in the right position without imitating him ; he points to the front and back vowels in order (i, e, ε, a) (u, o, ɔ, ɑ), waiting after each for the class to assume the right position and correcting faults.

He finally points to the symbols, one by one, but in any order, telling the class to put their lips in position for the symbol he is pointing to, and correcting as before.

The eight symbols are then written up on blackboard and numbered (B.B 3). The separate sounds are called out and the class is told to try to " spot " which sound is said, one by one.

1.	2.	3.	4.	5.	6.	7.	8.
i.	e.	ε.	a.	ɑ.	ɔ.	o.	u.

B.B.3.

LESSON 3.

3. The eight normal vowel-sounds : *Reproduction.*

" To-day we are going to practise the eight sounds we have already studied. But first let us run over the tongue- and lip-positions again "

The teacher then questions the class on the last two lessons He writes up the diagram of the eight sounds on the blackboard, working with the class and adding the sounds as the class explain them, one by one, starting from (i) to (a) and from (u) to (ɑ) ; the lip-positions are written up on the blackboard opposite

30   HOW TO TEACH FRENCH PHONETICS

each sound. The eight symbols are then numbered (white chalk) (B.B.1). The teacher makes sure that

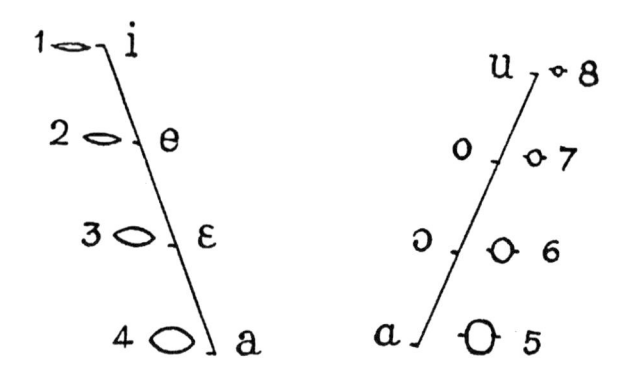

```
1 ⌒ ╲ i                    u ╱ ⌒ 8
2 ⌒ ╲ e                    o ╱ ⌒ 7
3 ⌒ ╲ ɛ                    ɔ ╱ ⌒ 6
4 ⌒ ╲ a                    a ╱ ⌒ 5
```

B.B.1.

the chart is understood thoroughly, both for the tongue and the lips. Ten minutes are given to this work.

" Now let us learn to make these sounds.

(i).

" First of all, there is no such sound as (ɪ) in French, as we find in the words ' it,' ' sit,' ' fit.' The French cannot say this sound; that is why they say (....) for ' it is difficult.' Now press your finger against your throat just under your chin and say ' it eats ' several times; do you feel any difference? The throat is tighter for ' eats ' than for ' it ' ? Well, in French the throat must be still tighter for (i)." The teacher says the English " see " and the French " si " to show the

FRENCH PHONETIC SYMBOLS 31

difference. The class then practise the sound, following the teacher, (i, i, i, i), etc. The class are told to keep the sound " tight " or " tense " and of course the correct lip-position is insisted on. (Glasses)

(e).

To obtain this sound it is best at first to tell the class to make no difference in the lip-position between (i) and (e). They should keep the lips in the (i) position, while imitating the sound (e) made by the teacher. This will counteract the tendency to move the lips as for (ei). The teacher says (i–e) (i–e) (i–e), etc., the class following him; they keep their eyes on the glasses to control their lips. There must be no lip-movement at all.

(u).

Starting from " fool " the class must push out their lips to a round pout and must keep them in this position while saying the sound; the opening should admit the sharp end of the pencil. In this position, and without any quivering, the class follows the teacher (u, u, u, u), etc. They control their lips all the time by their glasses.

(o).

To obtain this sound it is best at first to tell the class to make no difference in the lip-position between (u) and (o). They should keep their lips in the (u) position, while imitating the sound (o) made by the teacher. This will counteract the tendency to move the lips as for (ou). The teacher says (u–o) (u–o) (u–o), etc., the class following him; they keep their eyes fixed on their glasses to control their lips; there must be no lip-movement at all.

32 HOW TO TEACH FRENCH PHONETICS

(ε).

Starting from "get" the class is told to repeat (ε, ε, ε, ε) with the correct lip-position. The teacher repeats (i e—ε) (i e—ε), etc., with a clear drop between the (e) and the (ε); the class control their lips with the glasses.

(a).

"This sound is difficult to obtain. It does not exist in English (except in dialects); you must be careful not to mix it up with the English sound in 'cat,' 'pat,' 'hat' (æ), which sound does not exist in French. This French sound (a) is half way between our English sounds in 'pat' and 'part' (a, a, a, a)." To obtain a French sound of this description which is between two English sounds, it is a good plan to 'see-saw' between the two known sounds till the pupil hits on the correct sound. Thus, to obtain (a) the teacher will draw a line on the B B., placing (æ) on the top (pat), (ɑ) at the bottom (part), and the new French sound (a) (patte) in the middle (B.B.2). Saying first the words, he says "pat,

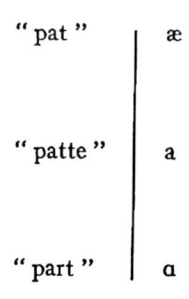

"pat"	æ
"patte"	a
"part"	ɑ

B.B.2.

FRENCH PHONETIC SYMBOLS

part, patte " several times, pointing to the top, the bottom and the middle as he says the corresponding sound. It will help the class to catch the right sound if the teacher says the two sentences "he patted him on the back" and "a cart went past" with the French (a) in the place of the English sounds. Then, pointing always to the sound he is saying the teacher isolates the sounds: "pat" (æ, æ, æ); "part" (ɑ, ɑ, ɑ); "patte" (a, a, a, a, a), etc, (æ, ɑ, a, a, a) (æ, ɑ, a, a, a, a), etc., (a, a, a, a, a, a). The class then practise the sound, aiming between (æ) and (ɑ), and controlling the lip-position with the glasses.

(ɑ).

This sound ought not to give much difficulty, the English (ɑ) as in " father " being a near enough equivalent. It is well to tell the class it is little used in French, No. 4 occuring more frequently than No 5. The class practise with glasses (ɑ, ɑ, ɑ), etc.

(ɔ).

This sound is a difficult one. To obtain it the " see-saw " method may be tried, aiming between " nut " and " not," with well-rounded lips. Another method is simply to try to say " nut " with rounded lips. This sound is perhaps better left until No. 11 (œ) has been taught,[*] and it ought not to be insisted on at this stage. The teacher will repeat (ɔ, ɔ, ɔ) and the class will control their lips with the glasses.

---

[*] No. 6 being between the French No. 11 and the English (ɔ) in " not ", and the French No. 11 being on the other side of the sound-chart.

34 HOW TO TEACH FRENCH PHONETICS

The class is then practised in the eight sounds, taking the four front and the four back ones together:

(i, e,–ɛ–a) (u, o,–ɔ,–ɑ),

the dash indicating a distinct drop of the jaw.

The following exercises are then done:

(i e) (i e) (i e) (i e), etc.
(u o) (u o) (u o) (u o), etc.
(i u) (i u) (i u) (i u), etc.,

the lip-position being if possible exaggerated and controlled by the glasses.

The lesson ends by the teacher reading through the eight sounds one by one in any order, and telling the boys to "spot" the number of the sound he says; finally he takes the sounds one by one, in any order, giving only the lip-positions, and asks the class to "spot" the sound he is saying.

LESSON 4.

4. *The mixed vowels.*

"To-day we shall learn three sounds that are called abnormal or mixed sounds. They are called mixed because they have the tongue position of front vowels but the lip-position of back vowels. We shall also learn an easy sound written (ə).

"What did we learn last time about the lip-position of the front vowels? And about the lip-position of the

FRENCH PHONETIC SYMBOLS

back ones?" The teacher gives ten minutes to recapitulation. (B B.1.)

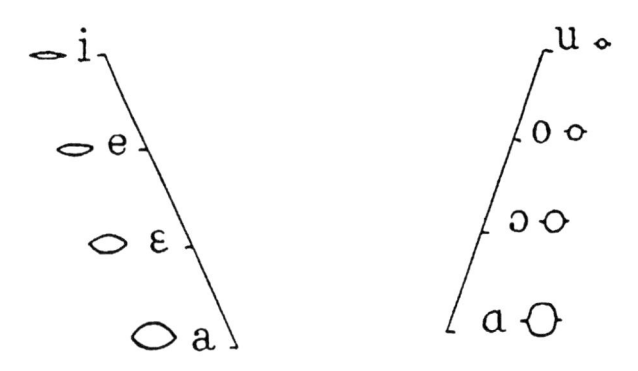

```
⊖i              u ○
 ⊖e              o ○
  ○ ɛ             ɔ ○
   ○ a             a ○
```

B. B. 1.

"Now look at the chart on the blackboard. I am going to say a sound you will recognise at once: (i). What sound was that? Good. You remember we are going to learn mixed sounds to-day. The first of these mixed sounds is made by saying (i), but with the lips rounded as for (u) instead of stretched. I am going to take a long breath and say (i) all the time, but I shall push out my lips while I am saying it, and you will hear that the sound becomes quite different." The teacher does so. "Now I shall say (i) and move my lips out and in and you will hear the sound changing back and forward." The teacher does so. "This new sound is

36 HOW TO TEACH FRENCH PHONETICS

written (y)." The teacher places it on diagram and repeats : (y, y, y). " It is quite easy to say once you know how it is formed.

" The next mixed sound is formed from (e) in the same way : that is to say you say (e) but stick out your lips in the position for (o)." The teacher repeats former process and writes up (ø). He repeats the sound several times.

" The third mixed sound is formed from (ε) in the same way : by saying (ε) and sticking out your lips as for (ɔ)." The teacher goes through same process as for (i–y) and writes in (œ) on the diagram.

The teacher explains why these sounds are placed where they are on the diagram : he then runs through the three sounds several times pointing them out as he is saying them. The teacher then teaches the sound (ə).

" We have now learnt twelve sounds, and we shall write them out in a row and number them   (B B 2)

1.	2.	3.	4.	5.	6.	7.	8.	9.	10.	11.	12.
i	e	ε	a	ɑ	ɔ	o	u	y	ø	œ	ə

B.B.2.

Now I shall say them through slowly several times, and then I shall call out different ones, and you must try to tell me the number of the sounds I say."

The teacher then exercises the class in " spotting " the numbers of the various sounds he calls out : he

FRENCH PHONETIC SYMBOLS

takes the twelve sounds one at a time, in any order. Mistakes are carefully distinguished by repeating the confused sounds together.

The teacher then goes through the twelve sounds, one by one, in any order, giving the lip-position only, and getting the class to " spot " the sound from the lip-position alone.

The rest of the lesson is given to practising the twelve sounds

As an example of this work the following exercises are given :—

(1) The teacher calls out single sounds in any order and the class assumes the correct lip-position for the sound given (glasses) :

(2) The four front vowels are read down (class following teacher) ; the four back vowels ditto (Great attention is given to the lips.)

(3) The mixed vowels are repeated from their base vowels (glasses).

2 and 3 are repeated several times (great care being given to correct lip-position, which is controlled by glasses) :

$$(i, e, -\varepsilon, -a) \ (u, o, -\mathit{\jmath}, -\alpha)$$
$$(i-y) \quad \text{also} \quad (i-y-u) \quad (u-y-i)$$
$$(e-\emptyset) \quad \text{also} \quad (e-\emptyset-o) \quad (o-\emptyset-e)$$
$$(\varepsilon-\textit{œ}) \quad \text{also} \quad (\varepsilon-\textit{œ}-\mathit{\jmath}) \quad (\mathit{\jmath}-\textit{œ}-\varepsilon)$$

38 HOW TO TEACH FRENCH PHONETICS

(4) The twelve sounds are then read through by the teacher, the class repeating each sound after him. (B.B 3)

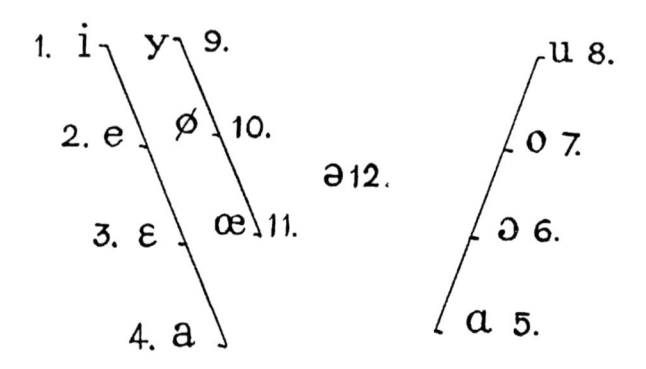

```
1. i     y  9.                    u 8.
2. e     ø  10.                   o 7.
                   ə 12.
3. ɛ     œ  11.                   ɔ 6.
4. a                              ɑ 5.
```

B.B.3.

(5) The teacher takes the difficult couples together, the class following him . (i–e) (u–y) (œ–ø) (ɛ–e), etc.

NOTE.—The device of forming (y) (ø) (œ) from (i) (e) (ɛ) respectively has been maintained here. It is, of course, not accurate But since we must start from a known sound, we have either to work up from (e) to (y) and from (ɛ) to (ø), or down from (i) to (y) and from (e) to (ø). For English pupils, whose vowel-sounds are usually too low, the latter method seems preferable. For (œ) the question is different, since we happen to have in English a sound (æ) which is phonetically nearer the true base sound of (œ) than (ɛ) is. We are inclined to think that quicker results will be obtained from (æ).

LESSON 5.

5. *The nasalised vowels.*

" We have so far learnt twelve vowel-sounds : to-day we shall learn four more, completing the total number of French vowel-sounds. The four sounds we have still to learn are called ' nasals ' because they are said through the nose.

" But let us begin by filling in the twelve sounds we already know on the chart " The teacher then writes up the twelve sounds in a line, numbering them, and runs through the tongue- and lip-positions of each as they are written separately in, on the chart. The class should be made to do this work on the blackboard, writing in forward and back vowels first, adding the lip-positions opposite each, then the mixed vowels and (ə). Ten minutes should be given to this recapitulation.

" The four new sounds are not new positions : they are made by taking four of the sounds you already know and saying them through the nose. The position of the lips and mouth is the same ; the only difference is that the air is now allowed to pass through the nose as well as through the mouth. The sounds thus changed are : (ɛ) (ɑ) (o) (œ)." The teacher tells the class to listen to him and to notice that he does not in any way change the position of his mouth, and then he repeats slowly the pairs . (ɛ–ɛ̃) (ɑ–ɑ̃) (o–õ) (œ–œ̃) several times.

The teacher then explains the action of the uvula in forming these sounds by drawing the diagram on the

B.B.1. Arrow indicates passage of air.

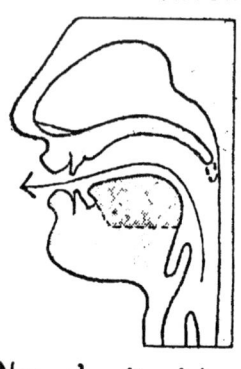

Normal soft palate position for ɛ.ɑ.o.œ.

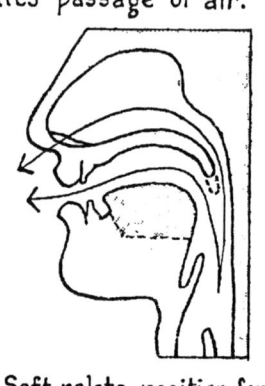

Soft palate position for nasalised ɛ̃.ɑ̃.õ.œ̃.

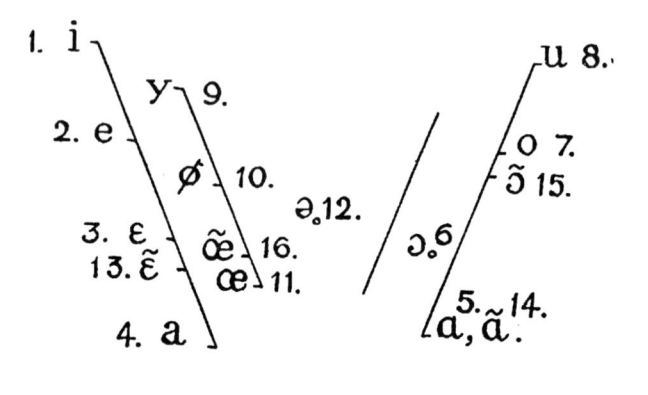

1. i
2. e
3. ɛ
13. ɛ̃
4. a

y 9.
ø 10.
œ̃ 16.
œ 11.

ə 12.
ɔ 6.

u 8.
o 7.
õ 15.
5. ɑ, ɑ̃ 14.

B.B.2.

blackboard. (B.B.1.) He draws the nasals in on the diagram. (B.B.2 as for full chart.) The teacher then repeats the sounds one after the other, always beginning from the base vowel (a–ã) (o–õ), etc. ; and gets the class to repeat them after him As always, they must work with the glasses, and should be particularly warned not to move the position of the mouth

The teacher then writes up the nasals at the end of his row of symbols, numbering them 13, 14, 15, 16. He practises these sixteen sounds as before, by reading them through slowly, pointing out each sound as he says it. (B.B.3.)

1. 2. 3. 4. 5. 6. 7. 8. 9. 10. 11. 12. 13. 14. 15. 16.
i e ɛ a ɑ ɔ o u y ø œ ə ɛ̃ ɑ̃ ɔ̃ œ̃

B.B.3.

With all the 16 symbols now on the board, the teacher can turn to the exercises given in Part II. and choose any exercises he thinks suitable for practising these sounds.

The exercises are arranged in two series :—

A   Ear-training exercises (for recognising sounds).

B.   Articulation exercises (for reproducing sounds).

and the teacher would do well to make these series alternate in his lessons

During these exercises, and those that follow before the consonants are taken, the teacher should keep a record of the sounds which cause particular difficulty to particular pupils To control individual progress, the eliminatory exercise (A.14) is recommended, with

42 HOW TO TEACH FRENCH PHONETICS

subsequent regrouping of the class, placing the weakest pupils in front. Where the system of five pupils in a row is adopted, the best pupil in the row should be placed in the middle and should be encouraged to help the weaker ones.

This lesson might be concluded in several different ways, the following will serve as alternative examples (30 min.) :—

A.1 (5 min.) or A 2 (5 min.) or A 1 (5 min.)
B.1 (10 ,,)   B.3 (10 ,,)   B.8 (10 ,,)
A.3 (10 ,,)   A.7 (15 ,,)   A.4 (10 ,,)
B.2 (5 ,,)   B.3 (5 ,,)

THE CONSONANTS MUST NOT BE ATTACKED UNTIL 50% CAN BE GAINED IN QUESTIONS ON THE VOWELS.

BETWEEN LESSON 5 AND LESSON 6 A PERIOD OF PRACTICE WILL THEREFORE BE NECESSARY.

THIS PERIOD WILL BE FILLED BY EXERCISES IN EAR-TRAINING AND ARTICULATION.

THE TEACHER WILL CHOOSE HIS EXERCISES FROM THE SERIES
    (1) "A," EAR-TRAINING.
    (2) "B," ARTICULATION.

HE WILL MAKE THESE SERIES ALTERNATE, IN EACH LESSON, ACCORDING TO THE NEEDS OF HIS CLASS.

A SAMPLE SELECTION OF EXERCISES FOR THE FIVE NEXT PERIODS IS GIVEN ON THE NEXT PAGE.

FRENCH PHONETIC SYMBOLS

EACH PERIOD LASTS 45 MINUTES.

First Period.
- A.1 (5) (Numbers in brackets refer to minutes)
- B.1 (10)
- A.3 (10)
- B.2 (10)
- A.5 (10)

Second Period.
- A.1 (5)
- B.1 (10)
- A.2 (10)
- B.4 (5)
- A.7 (15).

Third Period.
- B.1 (10)
- A.5 (10)
- B.6 (8)
- B.5 (2)
- A.10 (15).

Fourth Period.
- A 1 (5)
- B.3 (10)
- A.4 (10)
- B.7 (5)
- A.7 (15).

Fifth Period.
- B.1 (10)
- A.5 (10)
- B.8 (5)
- A.10 (20).

LESSON 6

6. *The Plosives*

" We have now gone through the French vowels—to-day we shall start on the consonants.

" What are vowels ? And what are consonants ? As a general way of distinguishing them we said vowels were sounds we could sing, while consonants were sounds we could not sing—is this strictly true ? Can we sing all the vowels—yes. Can we sing ' p,' ' s,' or ' f ' ?—No. But are there no consonants we can sing ? What about ' b,' ' z,' or ' v,' etc. ?

" So we see the consonants are of two kinds : those in which the voice is used, as part of the sound, and those in which the voice does not come in at all. The first are called ' voiced ' and the second ' unvoiced '."

The teacher gives examples, telling the class to feel if there is voice by holding the " Adam's apple " He explains the sign ($_\circ$)—(ɑ̃:ᴋʀ̥) (ɔ̃:ᴋl̥), etc.

" Now many consonants go in pairs, one is just the same as the other, except that the humming of the voice is added. Is there any voice in ' p ' ? Who can give me the voiced form ? " The same for t, d, and k, g.

" Now watch my lips while I say these sounds." The teacher says the six plosives, and elicits that the mouth closes and opens for each : he then says a fricative (s, f, z, etc.) to emphasise the fact that the plosives are different from the others " These six sounds are called ' plosives ' because the mouth has to shut and open with an explosion of breath in order to say them.

FRENCH PHONETIC SYMBOLS

" To-day we shall talk about these six sounds (p, b : t, d : k, g)."

The teacher then explains the difference between the French and English " p, b, t, d " (" k " and " g " may be left as in English). The English (p^h) (t^h) must be avoided. The best way to demonstrate the difference is to take a sheet of paper and hold it up in front of the face so that the bottom corner hangs about an inch in front of the mouth. If the teacher then says " papa " and " tata," in the English way, the corner will be distinctly blown away; if said with the French (p) and (t) there should be no movement at all.

To practise these sounds :

(1) they should be said very softly ;

(2) try to get between " pa " and "ba " ; " ta " and " da " ;

(3) hold the breath, to get the right " feel."

It is important that (b) (d) (g) should be fully voiced from the start.

The class should be exercised in pronouncing the unvoiced sounds, which will be a new experience for most of them. It is of course essential to insist on the correct pronunciation of these unvoiced consonants from the beginning.

When this distinction is clear the class may be exercised by writing up the six plosives on the B.B. in a row, and then saying them through with the different vowels (i, e, ɛ, a, u, ɔ, o), etc. The columns should be

46 HOW TO TEACH FRENCH PHONETICS

said first horizontally and then perpendicularly (B.B.1).
(Drills 1 & 2.)

B.B.1.

pi	bi	ti	di	ki	gi
e	e	e	e	e	e
ɛ	ɛ	ɛ	ɛ	ɛ	ɛ
a	a	a	a	a	a
u	u	u	u	u	u
o	o	o	o	o	o
i	i	i	i	i	i
y	y	y	y	y	y
e	e	e	e	e	e
ø	ø	ø	ø	ø	ø
ɛ	ɛ	ɛ	ɛ	ɛ	ɛ
œ	œ	œ	œ	œ	œ

The class should end by practice in the vowel-sounds as before. (Series A and B.)

LESSON 7.

7 *The Fricatives.*

"What was the great division of the consonant-sounds we found out in our last lesson ? How many sounds did we take last time ? Why six ? What were they called ? " etc. The teacher gives some time to recapitulation, and especially to making sure the class understands, and *pronounces* the unvoiced forms correctly. He elicits the reason why the " plosives " are so called.

FRENCH PHONETIC SYMBOLS

"To-day we shall take six other sounds which also go in pairs like the last six—three unvoiced sounds, each of which has a voiced form as well.

"The three unvoiced sounds are (f) (s) (ʃ) : who can give me the voiced forms?" The teacher elicits (v) (z) (ʒ). "These are called 'fricatives'."

"Are these like the 'plosives'? Why not? What is the difference?" The teacher elicits that the mouth does not open and shut, but that the sound goes on all the time; this can be easily demonstrated by telling the class to hum the two kinds of *voiced* sounds—plosives and fricatives (b, b, b : z——).

The teacher then explains the fricatives, and why so-called, etc. They are "rubbed" sounds. He lays special stress on the voiced forms, and emphasises the importance of fully voicing them when finals (vœ : v) (bɑ : z) (ʒy . ʒ).

These fricatives should be carefully practised alone and then in combination with vowel-sounds, as was done for the plosives. The teacher will write them up on B.B. in a row, and take them through with the various vowels, first across and then down the columns (B.B 2). (Drills 3 and 4.)

B.B.2.

ʃi	ʒi	si	zi	fi	vi
e	e	e	e	e	e
ɛ	ɛ	ɛ	ɛ	ɛ	ɛ
a	a	a	a	a	a
u	u	u	u	u	u
o	o	o	o	o	o

48 HOW TO TEACH FRENCH PHONETICS

B.B.2.—*continued.*

i	i	i	i	i	i
y	y	y	y	y	y
e	e	e	e	e	e
ø	ø	ø	ø	ø	ø
ɛ	ɛ	ɛ	ɛ	ɛ	ɛ
œ	œ	œ	œ	œ	œ

The last part of the lesson should be given to the vowel exercises (Series A and B).

LESSON 8.

8. *The Nasals.*

" What two different kinds of consonant-sounds have we learned so far ? " Plosives and fricatives. " What is the difference between them ? Why were they placed in pairs ? " etc. The teacher gives some time to recapitulating the two last lessons.

" To-day we shall learn three new consonant-sounds." The teachers says (m) (n) (ɲ) : " What sort of sounds would you call those ? " He elicits " nasals " ; if the class cannot "spot" they are nasals, the teacher will tell them to hold their nòses while saying them, when of course they will at once come to a stop.

The teacher then practises the class with (m) and (n), getting them well voiced. But for practical purposes the English sounds will do for the present. He will give most of his attention to (ɲ).

FRENCH PHONETIC SYMBOLS

To obtain (ɲ):

Start from English " onion ";

press the top of the tongue down to the roots of the lower front teeth and the tongue itself up against the hard palate ;

practise with various vowels (as below) keeping the tip well down.

If a pupil has particular difficulty in getting this sound the English sound in " onion " may be allowed to pass, for many French people pronounce it (nj).

These nasals should be exercised as the plosives and the fricatives. (B.B.3.) (Drill 5.) The exercises for the plosives and the fricatives should be gone through again. (Drills 1 to 4.)

B.B.3.

nɛ	ɲɛ	mɛ
a	a	a
ɑ	ɑ	ɑ
ɔ	ɔ	ɔ
o	o	o
u	u	u
i	i	i
y	y	y
e	e	e
ø	ø	ø
ɛ	ɛ	ɛ
œ	œ	œ

The lesson should end by some vowel exercises (Series A and B).

50 HOW TO TEACH FRENCH PHONETICS

LESSON 9.

9. (l) *and* (r).

" To-day we have two difficult sounds to learn : (l) and (r).

(l).

The teacher explains the dark and the clear (l) ; this is best done by giving words like " feel "—" feeling " ; " boil-boiling " ; where the dark (l) changes into the light one.

When the difference has been clearly heard, the class should be made to practise the clear form.

This can be done by

(1) Isolating the sound (fee–l) ;

(2) making it sound like (il) and not like (iəl) ;

(3) keeping the tip of the tongue between the teeth and saying (l) while putting before it all the vowel-sounds one after the other.

(r).

The lingual (r) should be taught except where the pupil finds the uvular one easier.

To teach the lingual (r) in cases where the pupil cannot say it :

(1) Start from English (r) and jump at it with strong emphasis ;

(2) start from English (r), and put " t " or " d " in front of it ;

FRENCH PHONETIC SYMBOLS

(3) try to get it unvoiced ;

(4) repeat (t–d) with increasing rapidity.

To teach uvular (R) :

(1) Start from (x) in Scotch " loch " ;

(2) voice this and practise the trill ; or

(3) gargle, reducing the quantity of water till there is none.

Drills 1, 2, 3, 4, 5 should now be done in full, across and down. (l) and (r) should be exercised similarly (B.B.4). The rest of the lesson should be given to vowel-exercises (Series A and B).

B.B.4.

rɛ	lɛ
a	a
ɑ	ɑ
ɔ	ɔ
o	o
u	u
i	i
y	y
e	e
ø	ø
ɛ	ɛ
œ	œ

Drills 11 and 19 should be added to the exercises on (r) and (l) at the next lesson ; the difficulty of final (r), especially after (u) and (i), and of final (l) being explained; also unvoiced final (r) and (l).

LESSON 10.

10. *The Semi-vowels.*

"We have three other sounds to learn in order to complete the total list of French sounds. They are called "semi-vowels."

"It often happens that one of the vowel-sounds (u) (i) or (y) occurs immediately in front of another vowel; when this happens they are not sounded to their full value, but change into consonants, *i e* they do not form a separate sound from the vowel that follows, but join on to it, so as to form one syllable instead of two.

"In such cases (u) is written (w),
               (i) ,, ,, (j),
               (y) ,, ,, (ɥ)."

This difference may be learnt from dictation of nonsense-words; the teacher will give combinations such as (sɛ–lu–i) (tapping out the three syllables) and (sɛ–lwi) (tapping out the two syllables); and similarly for (bɑ–li–o) (bɑ–ljo); (fo–sy–i) (fo–sɥi).

With pupils who already know French it may be pointed out that:

"joueur" is pronounced
      (ʒwœːr) (1 syll.) and NOT (ʒu–œːr) (2 syll.),

"lion" is pronounced
      (ljɔ̃) (1 syll.) and NOT (li–ɔ̃) (2 syll),

"puis" is pronounced
      (pɥi) (1 syll) and NOT (py–i) (2 syll.), etc.

(w) will not present any difficulty.

FRENCH PHONETIC SYMBOLS 53

(j) will require practice; the single syllable must be insisted on (bien, lion, etc.).

It occurs also after a vowel (ail, soleil, feuille, fille, etc.) and between two vowels (caillou, etc.).

(ɥ) is very difficult to learn; the usual method is to employ the vowel at first (puis being pronounced (pyi) and then to reduce the sound by practice to (ɥ) (pɥi), as a single syllable. (pwi) must be avoided at all costs.

These semi-vowels are practised (Drills 20 and 21).

The class then repeat drills 1, 2, 3, 4, 5; they practise final (r) and (l), (Drills 11 and 19); they repeat Drills 20 and 21.

Vowel-exercises from Series A and B.

THE CHIEF FAULTS TO BE CORRECTED IN THOSE WHO HAVE LEARNT FRENCH WITHOUT PHONETICS.

It usually happens that phonetics are introduced into a school as the result of a general organisation of the French side, and that they have to be taught, in all but the lowest forms, to pupils who have acquired a bad pronunciation. Especially in the higher forms will this faulty pronunciation have become habitual. It will often be found, as a consequence, that after learning the correct sounds the pupils will revert to

54 HOW TO TEACH FRENCH PHONETICS

their former mistakes, as soon as they get back to their reading books. This result is unavoidable at first, but it can be largely obviated if the pupils are given a list of the mistakes they are most likely to make, with a view to anticipating them in their class-preparation.

The following list should prove useful for this purpose.

VOWELS.

1. (i) : Substituting the English sound in " sit "— this will be especially likely to happen in a word which is written as in English (misérable, visiter, limite).

    Making the sound long (" see " for the short Fr. " si ").

2. (e) : Dipthonging (ei), especially in finals (nez, parler).

    Substituting (ɛ) as in " get " (défini, précieux).

    Substituting (i) as in " sit " (pénétrer, pétition).

3. (ɛ) : Substituting (ɛi) when final and long (lait, même).

    Changing quality before (r) : (fer, terre, clair).

4. (a) : Substituting (æ) as in " hat " when short and followed by a consonant (jamais, canne, cacher).

    Substituting (ɑ) when final (là, chat) and when followed by (r) (carte, garder, partir).

    Substituting (ə) in unaccented syllables (travailler, Italie).

5. (ɑ) : Substituting this sound for (a) : it is seldom used (parler, oiseau).

FRENCH PHONETIC SYMBOLS

6. (ɔ) . Substituting (ɔ:) as in "all" (Paul, augmenter) when long, and when followed by (r) (port, alors).
Substituting (ə) (commencer, prononcer, and correct).
Substituting (ɒ) as in English "not" when short and followed by a consonant (robe, poche).

7. (o) : Dipthonging (ou) ; the lips must not move.

8. (u) : Making it long at the end of a word (loup, poule).
Substituting short English (u) : (moustache, bouquet).
Adding (ə) before (r) : (lourd, tour).

9. (y) : Substituting (u), especially after (ʃ) (ʒ) (r) and plosives : (chute, juger, rue, publique, bureau).
Substituting (ju) : (vue, une, fumer, musique).

10. (ø) : Substituting (ə:) as in "bird" : (feu, feutre).

11. (œ) : Substituting (ə:) as in "bird" : (peur, beurre).

12. (ə) : Mistakes as to when to use it or leave it out.

13. (ɛ̃) : Making it too "tinny" : (vin, plein).

14. (ã) : Not opening the mouth sufficiently, especially after a labial (enfant, tremblement) : *i.e.* saying a sound more like (õ) than (ã).
Inserting a nasal consonant when followed by a plosive : (anglais (ã:glɛ) and not (ãŋglɛ) : tremper, (trã:pe) and not (trãmpe)).

56 HOW TO TEACH FRENCH PHONETICS

15. (ʒ) : Making it muffled and not clear.
Inserting a nasal consonant when followed by a plosive : (tomber (tɔ̃–be) and not (tɔ̃mbe) : monter (mɔ̃:te) and not (mɔ̃nte)).
16. (œ̃) : Confusing it with (ɛ̃) : (bien (bjœ̃) instead of (bjɛ̃), etc.).

CONSONANTS.

Plosives : Aspirating like in English (p^h) (t^h) (k^h).
Not sufficiently voicing (b) (d) (g).

Fricatives : Not sufficiently voicing final (v) (z) (ʒ).

Nasals : Substituting (nj) for (ɲ).

Labials : Substituting the dark (l) for the clear one before a consonant and when final : (ville, calmer).

Lingual (r) : Omitting before a consonant (aʀbre, paʀler).
Substituting (ə) for (r) when final (tour (tu:r) and not (tuə) : pir (pi:r) and not (piə)).

SEMI-VOWELS.

Pronouncing (j) like (i) : thus making two syllables of such words as " lion " and " bien " instead of only one syllable.

Pronouncing (ɥ) like (w) : thus making " lui " the same as " Louis." Too long : thus making two syllables of " lui."

PART II.

CLASS-ROOM EXERCISES IN FRENCH PHONETICS.

(A) EAR-TRAINING EXERCISES.

(B). ARTICULATION EXERCISES.

(C). SOUND DRILLS.

(D). PRELIMINARY EXERCISES IN PHONETIC READING AND DICTATION.

(A). EAR-TRAINING EXERCISES.

BLACK-BOARD
(For all Ear-Training Exercises.)
NUMBERED SYMBOLS — *(Yellow Chalk).*

1. 2. 3. 4. 5. 6. 7. 8. 9. 10. 11. 12. 13. 14. 15. 16.
i e ɛ a ɑ ɔ o u y ø œ ə ɛ̃ ɑ̃ ɔ̃ œ̃

EAR-TRAINING EXERCISES

(B.B. *Numbered Symbols.*)

(A.1). The teacher reads through the sixteen vowel-symbols slowly, repeating each one several times and pointing to each as he says it.

(i, i, i, i, i, i)
(e, e, e, e, e, e)
(ɛ, ɛ, ɛ, ɛ, ɛ, ɛ), etc.

He repeats the sixteen symbols saying each one once only—(i, e, ɛ, a, ɑ, ɔ), etc.

(A.2). The teacher reads through the sixteen symbols (as for A.1), and then takes (in couples) the sounds likely to be confused.

60 HOW TO TEACH FRENCH PHONETICS

Pointing to No. 1 he says—" this is (i, i, i)," and then pointing to No. 2—" this is (e, e, e)"; then he points first to 1 and then to 2, saying (ı, e) (i, e) (ı, e).

He deals in this way with all the pairs difficult to distinguish—writing them on the blackboard as he distinguishes them, thus:—

i	—	e
a	—	ɑ
ø	—	œ
ɔ	—	ɑ
u	—	y
i	—	y
e	—	ɛ
ɑ̃	—	ɔ̃
ɛ̃	—	œ̃
ɔ	—	œ

(A.3). The teacher, standing in front of the class so that his mouth can be seen, calls out a sound and the class must try to " spot " which it is by calling out its number in chorus.

A pupil must not be allowed to have more than one " shot."

The teacher immediately corrects any wrong answers. If he has given (e) some of the class will have said " No. 3." He will ask—" hands up those who say it is 3 ! " Then he will say—" Listen now, carefully," and, pointing to 2, he will say—" This is the sound I gave: (e, e, e) , No. 3 is (ɛ, ɛ, ɛ)," pointing to it ; then, pointing to No. 2 and No 3 alternately, he will say (e-ɛ) (e-ɛ) (e-ɛ).

He will treat all mistakes in this way..

EXERCISES IN FRENCH PHONETICS

(A.4). This exercise is exactly the same as A.3., except that the master stands *at the back* of the class so that his mouth cannot be seen.

The class are told to keep their eyes fixed on the blackboard.

This exercise is a better test for the ear than the last, as many pupils judge between like sounds by watching the teacher's lips.

(A 5). The teacher, standing in front of the class, calls out any symbol and the top pupil must at once try to " spot " the sound by calling out its number.

The other pupils are told to hold up their hand if they *disagree* with his answer.

Each sound taken is corrected separately (as above in Ex. 3).

The next sound is asked to pupil No. 2, and so on quickly round the class.

Great care is taken to correct sounds of which the class is not certain, by comparing them together and saying them in couples several times, pointing to each symbol as said.

All such confused symbols should be written up on the blackboard, and taken separately over a second time when the last pupil has had his turn.

(A.6). This exercise is exactly similar to No. 5 except that the teacher stands *behind* the class, who are told to keep their eyes on the blackboard.

Correcting on blackboard as before.

62 HOW TO TEACH FRENCH PHONETICS

(A.7). Dictation of separate vowel-sounds.

The teacher, after distributing paper, calls out ten sounds, saying each sound distinctly three times (at first, but later only once), and the class write down their symbols.

The teacher stands in front of the class.

Papers are then exchanged.

The teacher writes correct symbols up on blackboard.

Papers are corrected and marked, and marks are given up. (Papers should be collected and left on the teacher's desk for control.)

This exercise can be lengthened out if desired by having the papers returned to their writers, instead of collecting them after marking, and going through the ten sounds on blackboard for mistakes. The teacher asks for—"hands up those who got the first sound wrong," and then corrects the mistakes (as above in No. 3), going through all the ten sounds in this way.

Before rubbing the sounds off the board, the teacher will say them through, the class repeating after him; then the class will read them through in chorus alone.

(A.8). This exercise is the same as No. 7 except that the teacher stands *behind* the class while dictating the ten sounds.

(A.9). (This exercise should be used as soon as the class have learnt the consonants : *i.e.* after learning the plosives, nonsense words with (p, b, t, d, k, g) may be given ; (f, v, s, z, ʃ, ʒ) being added as learnt, and so on for the nasals, and (l) and (r)).

EXERCISES IN FRENCH PHONETICS

The teacher dictates either—

(1) Five two-syllable, or
(2) Three three-syllable nonsense-words, the class writing them down in symbols.

Examples of such nonsense-words would be (pi–ty) (ko–rø) (fa–se) (mi–y–pã) (tɛ–tɪ–te), etc. It is well to separate the syllables by a hyphen.

At first each of these nonsense-words should be repeated clearly *at least five times*. Later the teacher should say each twice, and finally only once. The pupils ought to be able to get 80% right (when said only once), to be satisfactory.

This dictation of nonsense-words is one of the best exercises, but its value lies in the care taken in correction. Let us suppose the first word is (mi–y–pã).

The teacher says this clearly five times, and gives the class time to get it down.

He then goes to the blackboard and asks—

"What is the first sound?" *Blackboard.*
  (Class answer " m.")
" and the second? " " i " ┌─────────────┐
  (He writes down " mi.") │ m i – y – pã │
                           └─────────────┘
" What was the third sound?" " y "
  (Writes it in.)
" And the fourth?" " p "
" And the last?" " ã "
  (Writes in " pã.")

F

64 HOW TO TEACH FRENCH PHONETICS

He does this quickly, taking the answers of the majority and ignoring—for the moment—the mistakes.

He then asks—" Hands up those who had ' mi ' wrong ? "

He then asks the pupils who hold up their hands, in order—" What symbol did you put ? " If the first pupil says " e," the teacher asks if any others made the same mistake. Usually the mistakes take one or two forms, and they can be quickly disposed of.

The teacher then says to the pupils who had put " me "—" Now I shall say the word as you have written it," and he writes " me " on the blackboard over " mi."

Blackboard.

```
m e –
m i – y – pã
```

Then, pointing to " me," he says : " (me–y–pã)," and pointing to (mi) " (mi–y–pã) " ; he repeats this several times, always pointing to the sound he is saying :, (me–y–pã), (mi–y–pã) (me–y–pã, mi–y–pã), etc., till the class clearly hear the difference.

He then asks for any other mistakes in the first syllable and treats them similarly, rubbing out (me) and placing over (mi) whatever false symbol has been given.

He repeats this with each syllable of the word, and he goes through all the words given in the same way.

EXERCISES IN FRENCH PHONETICS

This exercise takes up some time, but it is invaluable for improving the class in the recognition of the sounds.

With practice, the teacher will get through three words thoroughly in ten minutes. Where (as sometimes happens) a pupil has made an absurd mistake (putting a nasal for (i), etc.), it should be disregarded. Only those mistakes which are natural confusions should be written up on the blackboard and practised.

The teacher should grade the difficulty of the words given according to the growing capacity of the class.

After the first word has been corrected, the teacher should ask: " Hands up those pupils who had it quite right ? " After the second—" Hands up those who had both words right ? " and so on. At the end he should ask for a show of hands for those—

(1) Who had no mistakes,

(2) Who had only one mistake, etc.

This adds to the keenness of the class.

It is much better at first, *not to mark* these dictations, and to correct each word separately after the class have got it down.

Dictation for marks should be postponed until the class can get a high percentage in the exercise.

For marking purposes, the teacher should dictate the nonsense-words and then have the papers exchanged; he then writes up the correct symbols on the blackboard; the pupils correct the papers, and give up the marks.

The papers may then be returned to their owners, and the words can be worked over, if desired, on the blackboard, as above.

66 HOW TO TEACH FRENCH PHONETICS

It is advisable, however, either to give the exercise as above, or, if given as dictation for marks, not to add the blackboard work differentiating the sounds.

(A.10). The teacher calls out ten sounds, saying each sound distinctly three times (at first, but later only once), and the class write down their symbols.

The teacher stands in front of the class.

Papers are then exchanged.

The teacher calls out a pupil to write up his symbols on the blackboard. He writes up all ten.

The teacher then takes the sounds one by one, asking any pupils who disagree with the symbol on the blackboard to hold up their hand.

He then lets the class correct the work right through, being careful to explain confusions of sounds in the usual way, by writing up the wrong and the right symbols side by side and repeating the two sounds several times together, pointing as he does so to the symbol he is saying.

(A.11). This exercise is identical with A.10 except that the teacher stands *behind* the class, who must look at the symbols on the blackboard while he calls out the sounds.

(A.12). A pupil is called out and is told to take the class. He calls out any ten sounds he likes.

The teacher sits in the pupil's place and writes down the symbols with the rest of the class. The teacher then writes the correct symbol up on the blackboard.

Papers are exchanged, corrected, and marks are given up as usual.

EXERCISES IN FRENCH PHONETICS

(A.13.) This exercise is the same as the preceding one, except that instead of the teacher writing up the symbols on the blackboard, he tells the pupil taking the class, to call out another pupil to write them on the blackboard.

Instead of exchanging and marking, the lesson is then continued by the teacher getting the class to correct the symbols, and differentiating them from the sounds confused for them, one by one, as before.

(A.14). *Eliminatory Exercise.*

Not more than ten minutes should be given to this exercise, so it may be found advisable to test only half the class at a time.

The teacher calls out one pupil at a time to come to the phonetic chart. He then says a sound to which the pupil must point—if the pupil fails to recognise the sound, he returns to his place—if successful he is given two more sounds.

Those who fail to get the three sounds correct are placed in the front of the class and are tested again at a future date.

This exercise should be used from time to time to control individual progress.

(A.15). *Eliminatory Exercise.*

This exercise must be taken quickly. The class is told to stand.

Beginning with the top pupil and going straight round the class the teacher calls out a sound, and, answering in .turn, the pupil questioned must at once give its number.

68 HOW TO TEACH FRENCH PHONETICS

Any pupil who fails must sit down and remain sitting. The teacher motions with his hand for him to sit down, and passes on at once to the next pupil, giving another sound.

He runs through the class quickly three times, asking only the pupils who remain standing.

He then continues to ask those pupils who are still standing, for another round or two—those surviving at the end are declared winners.

(A.16). *Class Competition.*

The pupils are told to come to class each with one nonsense word of three syllables written down on a piece of folded paper. (They are most ingenious in discovering difficult combinations.)

Class divides—A and B.

The folded words are collected and placed in two bundles on the teacher's desk. (A and B.)

The teacher then selects three folded papers from A's bundle and three papers from B's bundle.

He dictates A's three words to B, and B's three words to A, giving one word first to one side, and then to the other.

Papers are then exchanged and marked.

The side with the least number of faults wins.

(B). ARTICULATION EXERCISES.

BLACKBOARD.

FOR ALL ARTICULATION EXERCISES, NUMBERED CHART.

Symbols in Yellow Chalk.

GLASSES are used for all these exercises.

(When not in use glasses are placed *face downwards* on the desks.)

ARTICULATION EXERCISES

(B.1). The teacher reads through the sixteen symbols in order, taking them one by one and getting the class to repeat each sound after him in chorus. (Glasses.)

He repeats each several times (i, i, i) (e, e, e), etc., and insists on the correct lip-positions.

The more difficult sounds are repeated over again and again until a fairly good result is obtained from the class.

The teacher will soon learn to detect any pupil who is pronouncing badly, and should note what sounds give most trouble to particular pupils.

(B.2). *Silent Lip-exercise.*

The teacher points to the symbols in order, and the class must put their lips in the proper position for pronouncing each sound, as pointed to. (Glasses.)

The class must keep their lips in position till the teacher has corrected any pupils whose lips are incorrect, and must only return to the normal position when the teacher calls out " Relax ! "

(B.3). This exercise is the same as the last, except that the symbols are taken in any order.

(a) The teacher points to any symbols (say e, ø, ɛ̃, u, œ, a), and the class must at once place their lips in the right position for pronouncing the symbol pointed to (glasses). They keep their lips in position until the teacher calls out " relax."

(b) Later, the class should go from one position to the other direct without relaxing (*i.e.* if the class have lips placed for (i) and the teacher points to (u) they must go straight from (i) to (u) and remain with lips pouting, till the teacher points to another symbol, and so on).

The teacher will use his discretion as to whether he assists the class by moving his own lips or not. In the early stages the class will require his aid.

(B.4). The teacher reads through the following pairs, couple by couple, getting the class to repeat after him.

As always, lip-position is insisted on. (Glasses.)

$$
\begin{aligned}
&\text{i} - \text{e} \\
&\text{u} - \text{y} \\
&\text{i} - \text{y} \\
&\text{e} - \text{œ} \\
&\text{ɛ} - \text{œ}
\end{aligned}
$$

This is repeated several times.

EXERCISES IN FRENCH PHONETICS

(B.5). *Mouth-stretching Exercise.*

The class, exaggerating if possible the lip-movement, continues saying (i–a–y) (i–a–y) for two minutes. (Glasses.)

N.B.—SLOWLY AND WITH GREAT TENSENESS AND PRECISION.

(B.6). The teacher reads over all the sounds one by one, the class repeating each sound after him, not in chorus, but individually round the class. (Glasses.)

He goes quickly three times round the class (where there are 16 pupils, the symbols must be changed to prevent the same symbol coming a second time to the same pupil).

The teacher repeats the sound where a pupil fails to get it right, before passing on to the next pupil.

(B.7). Pupils sing the eight normal sounds slowly up and down the scale, several times—strong lip-movement. (Glasses.)

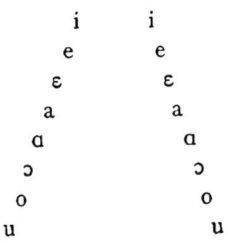

```
        i           i
       e           e
      ɛ           ɛ
     a           a
    ɑ           ɑ
   ɔ           ɔ
  o           o
 u           u
```

Before *singing* these sounds, the teacher *says* them through, up and down, followed by the class.

(B.8). *Chart Exercise.*

The teacher, pointing to symbols on chart, reads out—

(1) i–e–ɛ–a   (he makes *no* change in the opening of
Class repeat.   the mouth between (i)–(e), drops dis-
(i–e–ɛ–a)   tinctly for (ɛ), and further for (a).)

(2) u–o–ɔ–ɑ   (he makes *no* change in the opening of
Class repeat   the mouth between (u)–(o), dropping
(u–o–ɔ–ɑ)   distinctly for (ɔ), and further for (ɑ)).

(3) i–y.   (Class repeat.)
(4) e–ø.   (Class repeat.)
(5) ɛ–œ.   (Class repeat.)
(6) ɑ̃–ɔ̃.   (Class repeat.)
(7) ɛ̃–œ̃.   (Class repeat.)

This is repeated several times, great attention being given to correct lip-positions (glasses).

When the class know this exercise they will go through it by themselves, the teacher starting them off by calling out "Chart Exercise."

The teacher naturally corrects any pupils whose lip-position is faulty.

When proficient, the class should begin every lesson by saying this exercise quickly through without the aid of the teacher.

(B.9). The teacher, telling the class to look at the numbered chart, calls out a number, or points to a symbol, and the class must at once give the correct sound in chorus, retaining the lip-position till the teacher calls "relax!"

EXERCISES IN FRENCH PHONETICS

The teacher corrects wrong lip-positions, and then calls out another number, the class answering by the correct sound as before, in chorus, again retaining the lips in position.

The teacher again corrects wrong lip-position and continues this process till ten numbers have been called out (glasses).

The class must keep their lips in the correct position after they have called out the sound till the teacher, having corrected the pupils who are wrong, calls out "relax!"

Thus, if he gives No. 1, the class will answer (i), keeping their lips stretched. Supposing there are three pupils who have their lips insufficiently stretched the teacher calls out their names, tells them to stretch their lips more, and only when all the class have their lips correctly stretched, does he say "relax!"

The class then return their lips to the normal position.

If the teacher then calls out "8" the class will answer (u), and keep their lips pouted till the pupils who are wrong have got the right lip-position. The teacher then repeats the order "relax," and goes on to some other number.

The exercise must be taken smartly.

(B.10). *Eliminatory Exercise.*

This exercise must be taken quickly. Class is told to stand.

Beginning with the top pupil and going straight round the class the teacher points to a symbol on the chart and the pupil whose turn it is must at once call out the correct sound, with correct lip-position.

Any pupil who fails must sit down and remain sitting. The teacher motions with his hand for him to sit down, and passes on at once to the next pupil, pointing to another symbol.

He runs through the class quickly three times, asking only the pupils who remain standing.

He then continues to ask those still standing another round or two; the survivors being declared winners.

(C). SOUND-DRILLS.

These exercises will be repeated after the teacher: first across each line and then downwards in columns.

It is essential to remember that each of these vowel symbols represents a *lip-position* as well as a sound, and that the lips *must* be placed in the correct position for each sound before it is made.

The lips and tongue must remain steady for a few seconds after each syllable has been made.

C. (I.)

pi	bi	ti	di	ki	gi
pe	be	te	de	ke	ge
pɛ	bɛ	tɛ	dɛ	kɛ	gɛ
pa	ba	ta	da	ka	ga
pu	bu	tu	du	ku	gu
po	bo	to	do	ko	go

C. (II.)

pɪ	bi	tɪ	dɪ	ki	gi
py	by	ty	dy	ky	gy
pe	be	te	de	ke	ge
pø	bø	tø	dø	kø	gø

C. (III.)

ʃi	ʒi	sɪ	zɪ	fɪ	vi
ʃe	ʒe	se	ze	fe	ve
ʃɛ	ʒɛ	sɛ	zɛ	fɛ	vɛ
ʃa	ʒa	sa	za	fa	va
ʃu	ʒu	su	zu	fu	vu
ʃo	ʒo	so	zo	fo	vo

C. (IV.)

ʃi	ʒi	si	zi	fi	vi
ʃy	ʒy	sy	zy	fy	vy
ʃe	ʒe	se	ze	fe	ve
ʃø	ʒø	sø	zø	fø	vø

C. (V.)

rɛ	lɛ	nɛ	ɲɛ	mɛ
ra	la	na	ɲa	ma
rɑ	lɑ	nɑ	ɲɑ	mɑ
rɔ	lɔ	nɔ	ɲɔ	mɔ
ro	lo	no	ɲo	mo
ru	lu	nu	ɲu	mu

EXERCISES IN FRENCH PHONETICS

C. (VI.)

Great attention to be paid to final consonants.

bif	fɪt	lil	mil	kij
bys	fyt	lyp	myl	kyr
bev	fel	les	met	keʒ
bøf	føt	løp	møv	køs
bal	fat	lak	mat	kal
buk	fus	luf	mul	kut
bom	fot	lob	mov	kot

C. (VII.)

ʒit	ʃɪk	sɪl	pɪk	vil
ʒyʒ	ʃyl	sys	pys	byk
ʒel	ʃef	set	pen	ven
ʒøk	ʃøp	søl	pøt	vøt
ʒɛt	ʃɛk	sɛt	pɛl	vɛʒ
ʒak	ʃal	sal	pat	vaʃ
ʒup	ʃuʃu	sul	pur	vut
ʒon	ʃod	sos	pol	vom

C. (VIII.)

rɛk	nɛk	tɛt	kɛt
rɔk	nɔt	tɔl	kɔl
raʒ	nat	tak	kap
rut	nul	tus	kul
rol	not	toto	koko
ryd	nyl	tyl	kyrly

C. (IX.)

pã	pɔ̃	pɛ̃	pœ̃
tã	tɔ̃	tɛ̃	tœ̃
ʒã	ʒɔ̃	ʒɛ̃	ʒœ̃
mã	mɔ̃	mɛ̃	mœ̃
lã	lɔ̃	lɛ̃	lœ̃

C. (X.)

ʃã	ʒɔ̃	sɛ̃	zœ̃
fã	vɔ̃	rɛ̃	lœ̃
nã	mɔ̃	fɛ̃	sœ̃
ʒã	fɔ̃	mɛ̃	ʃœ̃
mã	nɔ̃	ʒɛ̃	rœ̃
vã	sɔ̃	nɛ̃	ʒœ̃
sã	ʃɔ̃	zɛ̃	vœ̃

C. (XI.)

The final " r." This exercise must be practised as follows :—With the exception of the vowel sounds " a " and " ɛ," the lip position of the final vowel sound must be kept while the " r " is being made, and should only be relaxed after the latter sound has died away.

iːr	sIːr	liːr	biːr	tiːr
pyːr	myːr	kyːr	lyːr	fyːr
ʒuːr	kuːr	tuːr	buːr	fuːr
ɔːr	fɔːr	kɔːr	sɔːr	mɔːr
œːr	mœːr	kœːr	lœːr	sœːr
aːr	baːr	faːr	raːr	maːr
klɛːr	sɛːr	vɛːr	tɛːr	mɛːr

EXERCISES IN FRENCH PHONETICS

C. (XII.)

riʃ	rim	rɪk	rika	rime	riʃəljø	rigɑ
re	rɛsɛl	reklam	rɛsɪ	regle	reʒi	reglis
rɛkto						
raba	rabɛ	rabo	rablɛ	rwajal	raʃa	rwatlɛ
rɑt	rɑpo	rɑto	rɑf	rɑkle	rɑl	rɑle
rudu	rubl	rule	rug	ruge		
roz	roze	aroze	rot	rotir		
rɔb	rɔbɛːr	rɔbɪnɛ	rɔʃ	rɔk	rɔʃe	
ryʃ	ryze	ryd	ryʒiːr			
rɔlɛ	rəlatif	ɪəljɛf	rəmiz			

br

C. (XIII.)

brɪg	brik	brɪz	brisk	brid		
brɛk	brɛf	brɛʃ	brɛv			
brak	brav					
bro	brɔʃ	brɔd	brɔs			
bru	bryʒ	brym	bryl	bryn	bryt	
brœl	brø	brijø	brige	brize		
broʃe	bruje	brizyːr				

80 HOW TO TEACH FRENCH PHONETICS

kr   C. (XIV.)

kri	krik	krim	
kre	kredi	kredo	kree
krɛ	krɛm	krɛf	krɛj
krak	kras	krasø	kratɛːr krwaze
krɑn	krwɑ		
krup	krupje	krɔʃy	
kry	kryʃ	krysifi	kryɛl
krø	krøːz	krøːze	

dr   C. (XV.)

drij	drijad		
drɛʃ	drɛs		
drak	dragm	draʒe	drapo
drwɑ			
dru	drue		
droːl	droːm		
drɔg	drɔge		
dry	drvp		
drø			

EXERCISES IN FRENCH PHONETICS

gr   C. (XVI.)

gri	grif	grim	grij	grɪːz	grize	grizu
gre	gree					
grɛb	grɛk	grɛs	grɛf	grɛg		
grat						
grɑv						
grop	grupe					
gro	gros					
grɔg	grɔt					
gry	grym	grymo	gryjeːr			

pr   C. (XVII.)

prɪ	prim	prɪme	primidɪ	primis		
pre	preo	presi	presɪte			
prɛʃ	prɛʃe	prɛsjø				
pralin	pratik	pratike				
prwɑ						
proz	prot	prote	proto			
prɔʃ	prɔb	prɔʃɛ̃	prɔʃil	prɔpo	prɔʒɛ	prɔprə
pryn	pryno	prynɛl	prys	pryd		
prø	prœːv					

C. (XVIII.)

lala	lak	lase	
lɛ			
li	lis	lizɪbl	lig
lyli	lyl	lyt	lyn
luːr	lu		

C. (XIX.)

bil	fɪl	sɪl
zɛl	mɛl	fɛl
mal	bal	sal
rɑl	mɑl	pɑl
fɔl	bɔl	sɔl
tol	rol	sol
kul	rul	mul
pilyl	pistyl	ʒyl
møl	gøl	øl
sœl	mœl	rœl

C. (XX.)

Semi-vowel " w."

wɪ	wa	wazo	twal	vwajɛl	mwal
vwal	lwi	lwa	blwa	mwa	rwa
walɔ̃	wist				

C. (XXI.)

Semi-vowel " ɥ."

ɥɪ	ɥɪt	ɥɪtɛ:n	ɥitjɛ:m	ɥɪsje	ɥilje
ɥɪtr	ɥitɲe	ɥitɲɛ:r	pɥɪ		
lɥi	tɥil	egɥi:j			

EXERCISES ON SEPARATE VOWEL SOUNDS.

C. (XXII.)

Vowel Sound No. 1, "i."

ʒi	ʒit	ʒivr	bigl	big	bil	bis
sibl	sidr	sıl	silıs	sım	sivık	difisıl
dig	dim	diːr	dısiplın	disk	distik	dis
district	divın	fibr	fıbrik	finı	fıktiv	fil
livr	lıvid	lıŋk	mil	mılis	mim	min
pık	pıːr	ki	kiȷ	kınin	riʃ	rısin
rid	rim	riːr	siɲ	silik	tiːʒ	tiːr
vıktim						

C. (XXIII.)

No. 2, "e."

bebe	sede	ble	de	fe	peʃe	repete
ebete	ne	ʒe	ʃe	prefere	kree	kle
ete	te	eple	pre	desede	delege	

C. (XXIV.)

No. 3, "ɛ."

frɛ	mɛ	rɛspɛ	rɛːd	pɛ	ɛl	mɛːr
pɛːr	vɛːr	tɛrn	pɛːz	sɛːm	mɛːm	
bɛʃ	frɛʃ	frɛl	nɛgr	pɛst	ʒɛst	
tɛt	pɛl	ʒɛl	grɛl	mɛl	mɛːn	
frɛːn	frɛːz	ʃɛːn	glɛb	glɛv	rɛːn	

C. (XXV.)

No. 4, " a."

aba	abatr	akabl	adapt	alg	akt	arab
bak	bag	barak	baɲ	bal	gam	mal
nap	trap	sak	lak			
ar	kaːv	kaːr	baːv	taːr	saːʒ	raːr
paːr	daːr	avwaːr	bwaːr	swaːr	laːv	
gaːr	barbaːr	ardwaːz				

C. (XXVI.)

No. 5, " ɑ."

bɑ	kɑ	tɑ	mɑ	bwɑ	mwɑ	trwɑ
vwɑ	kwɑ	pɑ	nwɑ	grɑ	glɑ	
ɑːm	kɑːbl	blɑːm	ɑːpr	krɑːb	fɑːbl	
mɑːl	lɑːʃ	tɑːʃ	tɑːs	klɑːs	lɑːs	pɑːs
ʒɑːk	pwɑːl	sɑːbl	sɑːbr	vɑːz	pwɑ	

C. (XXVII.)

No. 6, " ɔ."

rɔb	rɔs	sɔm	tɔʒ	tɔr	trɔ	
blɔk	bɔn	bɔk	bɔs	kɔl	kɔk	ʃɔk kɔʃ
kɔd	kɔfr	kɔt	dɔgm	dɔk	fɔk	fɔl
fɔks	fɔrs	gɔlf	glɔt	lɔk	mɔdr	non nɔt
pɔm	prɔb	rɔm				

C. (XXVIII.)

No. 7, "o."

bo	ʃo	do	fo	gro	lo	mo	no
po	so	to	tro	vo	grolo	rokoko	
doːm	koːn	droːl	foːʃ	foːt	ʒoːn		
goːfr	goːʃ	goːl	moːv	poːl	roːz		
soːs	soːv	soːl	troːn				

C. (XXIX.)

No. 8 (i), "u."

buk	bu	buʃ	kuʃ	kup	klu	kuku	krup
dus	fu	fudr	fug	gu	grup	gut	lu
lup	mu	muʃ	pul	pus	ru	rus	
tu	tus						

C. (XXX.)

No. 8 (ii), "u."

buːl	buːr	buːʒ	kuːr	kuːz	duːz
fuːr	ʒuːr	fuːl	luːvr	luːr	suːr
tuːr	ruːʒ	ruːvr	uːvr		

C. (XXXI.)

No. 9, "y."

by	byt	bryt	bry	bryn	klyb	
kry	kyb	dy	dyp	dyk	fy	
fyt	flyt	flyks	ʒyp	ʒy	lyn	byt
lyʒ	ny	nyl	pryn	pyʃ	pyrg	py
rys	sys	sukr	myːz	pyːr	syːr	
bys	dyːr	kyːr	kyːv	ʒyːʒ	myːr	

86 HOW TO TEACH FRENCH PHONETICS

C. (XXXII.)
No. 10, "ø."

ø	dø	sø	krø	fø	gø	3ø
nø	pø	prø	plø	vø		
krø:z	bø:gl	fø:tr	3ø:n	mø:t	nø:tr	

C. (XXXIII.)
No. 11, "œ."

œf	bœf	kœj	dœj	gœl	mœbl
nœf	pœpl	vœf			
œ:vr	kœ:r	bœ:r	flœ:r	lœ:r	
vœ:r	sœ:r	nœ:r	plœ:r	prœ:v	

C. (XXXIV.)
No. 14, "ɑ̃."

ɑ̃	bɑ̃	blɑ̃	dɑ̃	ʃɑ̃	gɑ̃	grɑ̃
glɑ̃	sɑ̃	rɑ̃	vɑ̃	vɑ̃tɑ̃	tɑ̃	tɑ̃tɑ̃
pɑ̃	ɑ̃:pl	kɑ̃:fr	lɑ̃:p	sɑ̃:bl	trɑ̃:p	
tɑ̃:p	tɑ̃:t	vɑ̃:t	fɑ̃:dr	ɑ̃:ʃ	tɑ̃:dr	
vɑ̃:dr	frɑ̃:ʒ					

C. (XXXV.)
No. 15, "ɔ̃."

ɔ̃	bɔ̃	dɔ̃	tɔ̃	mɔ̃	lɔ̃	fɔ̃
tɔ̃dɔ̃	bɔ̃dɔ̃	dɔ̃tɔ̃	tɔ̃tɔ̃	mɔ̃tɔ̃	lɔ̃ʒɔ̃	
rɔ̃:pr	rɔ̃:d	trɔ̃:p	sɔ̃:br	ʒɔ̃:ʃ	kɔ̃:t	
kɔ̃tɔ̃	mɔ̃:d	pɔ̃:s	plɔ̃:b	dɔ̃:t	ɔ̃:br	
frɔ̃:d	kɔ̃:bl	pɔ̃:p				

EXERCISES IN FRENCH PHONETICS 87

C. (XXXVI.)
Nos. 14 and 15, "ã, ɔ̃."

ɑ̃tɑ̃dɔ̃	tɑ̃tɔ̃	sɑ̃blɔ̃	mɔ̃tɑ̃	pɑ̃sɔ̃
ʒɔ̃ʃɑ̃	dɑ̃tɔ̃	kɔ̃tɑ̃	lɔ̃tɑ̃	vɑ̃dɔ̃
bɑ̃dɔ̃	bɔ̃dɑ̃	sɔ̃brɑ̃	ʃɑ̃tɔ̃	ɔ̃braʒɑ̃

C. (XXXVII.)
No. 13, "ɛ̃."

bɛ̃	dɛ̃	frɛ̃	fɛ̃	gɛ̃	nɛ̃	plɛ̃
vɛ̃	pɛ̃	tɛ̃tɛ̃	pɛ̃:tr	ɛ̃stɛ̃	sɛ̃:tr	
plɛ̃sɛ̃:tr	fɛ̃:dr	pɛ̃:s	nɛ̃:b	tɛ̃:dr		
nɛ̃:f	sɛ̃:pl	dɛ̃:d	sɛ̃:dr	rɛ̃tɛ̃tɛ̃		

C. (XXXVIII.)
No. 16, "œ̃."

| œ̃ | brœ̃ | ʒœ̃ | œ̃:bl | məlœ̃ | lœ̃di |

(D). PRELIMINARY EXERCISES IN PHONETIC READING AND DICTATION.

PRELIMINARY READING EXERCISES.

The following ten Exercises are arranged in logical order :—

        1. Single Sounds.
        2. Sound-groups.
        3. Breath-groups.

These various stages may be worked through in a single lesson. Where this is done it is advisable to change the text, *i.e.* to read through a phonetic text devoting the first two lines to 1, the second two lines to 2, the third two lines to 3, to avoid the monotony of constantly repeating the same lines.

In the text we have used the same example throughout, but this would naturally not be done in practice.

SINGLE SOUNDS.

(D.1). The teacher, telling the class to follow him with their eyes on their phonetic text, but to make no attempt to imitate him, reads a few lines of the text, sound by sound. He does *not* join up the sound-groups to form words or sentences.

Thus, supposing the phonetic text to be : (aprɛ lə supe, dɑ̃ le boʒuːr, ɔ̃ s asɛjɛ syr lə pɛrɔ̃), the teacher

EXERCISES IN FRENCH PHONETICS

would read out the sounds singly as they come—(a, p, r, ɛ, l, ə, s, u, p, e), etc., the class listening carefully and following the text in their own books as the teacher reads.

(D.2). The teacher, having read through the text once or twice, as in No. 1, tells the class to read each sound out softly in chorus, after him. Great care is taken with the consonants (unvoiced and voiced).

(D.3). The class is then told to read out each sound one by one, in chorus, without any aid from the teacher.

SOUND-GROUPS.

(D.4). The teacher reads through the text sound by sound, but at the end of each sound-group he will put the sounds together which form the separate words: thus, in the text given for No. 1 (aprɛ lə supe, dɑ̃ le boʒuːr), etc., he will read (a, p, r, ɛ,—aprɛ), (l, ə,—lə), (s, u, p, e,—supe), etc., and so on through the text.

The Class will be told to listen carefully, and to follow word for word in their texts, but not to attempt to imitate the teacher.

(D.5). The teacher, having read through the text once or twice as in No. 4, tells the pupils to repeat each sound and each sound-group after him, as he says it.

(D.6). The class is then told to read through the text in the same way (No. 5) in chorus, by themselves—first single sounds and then the various groups formed.

(D.7). The class is told to read through the text, sound-group by sound-group, by themselves; they would then read the above text as follows: (aprɛ – lə – supe – dɑ̃ – le – bo – ʒuːr), etc.

90 HOW TO TEACH FRENCH PHONETICS

BREATH-GROUPS.

(D.8). The teacher tells the class to follow, with their eyes on the text, and to listen carefully to him while he reads the text in breath-groups. Thus he would read the text given in (1) as follows : (aprɛləsupe – dɑ̃leboʒuːr – ɔsasɛjɛ – syrləperɔ̃). Although intonation need not be taught at this early stage, the teacher should nevertheless say these phrases naturally, and should avoid dropping into a dull monotone.

(D.9). The class is told to read these breath-groups out loud, in chorus, after the teacher.

(D.10). The class is allowed to read these breath-groups alone, in chorus, without any assistance from the teacher. Without conscious effort on their part they should be led to imitate the correct intonation of the teacher.

PRELIMINARY DICTATION EXERCISES.

Before giving a phonetic dictation to the class it is advisable to work through several dictations on the blackboard, the whole class assisting.

The teacher selects a short sentence—(lə ʒuːr sə diviːz ɑ̃ vɛ̃ːt katr œːr)—and, standing at the blackboard, repeats the sentence in small groups.

Thus he will say (ləʒuːr sə diviːz), and will repeat this phrase two or three times, then he will ask the class how many sounds occur in the first sound-group (ləʒuːr).

EXERCISES IN FRENCH PHONETICS

He elicits " ɔ̃," and then asks, what are they? He writes them on the blackboard separately as the class calls them out (l. ə, ʒ, u, r), and goes through each sound-group in this way. He will naturally correct any wrong suggestions. After each sound-group has been written up on the blackboard he will repeat it together— (l, ə, ʒ, u, r—" ləʒuːr "), etc.—and so on through all the sound-groups in the phrase he has called out.

When the first phrase—(lə ʒuːr sə diviːz)—has been dealt with in this way, and is correctly written up on the blackboard, the teacher will call out the next phrase— (ɑ̃ vɛːt katr œːr)—and work through the text chosen in this way.

It is important to ask the class to count the number of sounds they hear in any sound-group before writing them up on the blackboard, as this is good training for their ears and helps to avoid mistakes. A group such as (krwɑːje) will cause difficulty unless the class realises there are six different sounds in it.

Much time is gained by working through several dictations in this way on the blackboard, before giving the phonetic dictation in the usual manner, and many mistakes the class would otherwise have made may thus be avoided.

An occasional dictation done on the blackboard in this way, and then read over sound by sound, sound-group by sound-group, and finally breath-group by breath-group, as a reading exercise, will be found a good combination and a useful change.

No attention need be paid at this stage to length marks.

BIBLIOLIFE

Old Books Deserve a New Life
www.bibliolife.com

Did you know that you can get most of our titles in our trademark **EasyScript**™ print format? **EasyScript**™ provides readers with a larger than average typeface, for a reading experience that's easier on the eyes.

Did you know that we have an ever-growing collection of books in many languages?

Order online:
www.bibliolife.com/store

Or to exclusively browse our **EasyScript**™ collection:
www.bibliogrande.com

At BiblioLife, we aim to make knowledge more accessible by making thousands of titles available to you – quickly and affordably.

Contact us:
BiblioLife
PO Box 21206
Charleston, SC 29413